CLASSIC RECIPES FOR YOUR FAN OVEN

THEIR NEW TIMES AND TEMPERATURES

BY

SYLVIA FIGGINS

✳

foulsham

LONDON · NEW YORK · TORONTO · SYDNEY

foulsham

The Publishing House,
Bennetts Close, Cippenham, Berkshire, SL1 5AP, England.

ISBN 0-572-02323-5

Copyright © 1997 Sylvia Figgins
Cover photograph © Anthony Blake Photo Library

Typeset by ABM Typographics Ltd, Hull
Printed in Great Britain by St. Edmundsbury Press,
Bury St. Edmunds, Suffolk

CONTENTS

ACKNOWLEDGEMENTS

Thank you to my husband, who allowed me to use a variety of ovens at Home Affair (Kitchen) Studio for testing, and to Alex who typed the manuscript.

Without support and help from the following manufacturers it would have been impossible to complete this book. They gave me all the necessary information and allowed me to reproduce their recipes and, where possible, to use their ovens for testing.

AEG (UK) Ltd
Atag (UK) Ltd
Belling Appliances Ltd
Bosch Domestic Appliances Ltd
Creda Ltd
De Dietrich
Gaggenau (UK) Ltd
Imperial (UK) Ltd
Miele Ltd
Neff (UK) Ltd
Scholtes UK
Tricity Bendix
Zanussi Ltd

Also:
Britannia Appliances
Hotpoint Ltd
Stoves plc

INTRODUCTION

There is no doubt that a great deal of confusion surrounds fan ovens. Thousands of people own one or are about to buy one but very few know how to get the best out of it. In this book I will help you understand how a fan oven works and guide you into achieving results in ways no gas or conventional oven can offer. I will also explain the vast range of options on the most up-to-date 'multi-function' ovens.

As a mother of small children I have little time for lengthy preparation and last-minute finishing off before serving and this will be reflected in many of the recipes in this book. Convenience foods that can help to reduce preparation time are included in Cook's Notes. Convenience foods and ready-prepared meals play a large part in our lives and I give guidance on how long and at what temperature to cook them.

All of the recipes give guidance for cooking in the fan system. However, you can use a conventional oven by referring to the Temperature Chart on page 12 for the increase necessary in temperature and cooking time.

The variety of fan ovens available almost equals the number of different cars on the roads. Don't despair: I believe that, just as passing your test in one type of car enables you to adapt to driving many others, the basic guidelines in this book can equip you to cook in any fan oven, with a little back-up help from your manufacturer's instruction book!

SYLVIA FIGGINS

FAN OVENS AND FAN ASSISTED OVENS

What exactly is a fan oven?

The term 'fan oven' is misleading, because it can apply to any oven containing a fan within the oven. The type of oven I refer to in this book is really a 'forced air convection oven'.

Let me remind you of how a conventional oven works. A conventional oven has elements either in the sides or, like most ovens now, at the top and bottom – the outer edge of the grill element acting as the top source of heat, the base element being concealed. These elements take time to heat up, resulting in a 15–20 minute preheating period before the thermostat light goes out and cooking can commence. The oven relies on the natural circulation of hot air to cook the food and, because hot air rises, cooking on more than one shelf involves a lot of moving around to obtain even cooking.

In a forced air convection oven there is an element around the fan at the back of the oven but, instead of blowing out hot air as a hair drier would, the fan draws air in across the element, then pushes the heated air down the sides of the oven and, in some cases, under and over the back panel before repeating the process. Of course, oven designs do vary, but this constant, **controlled** circulation of hot air released into the oven at different points is the key to all the many advantages of true fan cooking.

Warm air begins to circulate in the oven immediately, and so it is possible in many cases, to place food in the oven without preheating. Even if preheating is required, it is only necessary to set the oven temperature for 5–8 minutes before placing the food in the oven – just sufficient for warm air to have circulated thoroughly around the oven. It is not necessary to wait for the thermostat light to go out.

Most manufacturers have their own patented name for their particular fan system but the basic principles of cooking are the same.

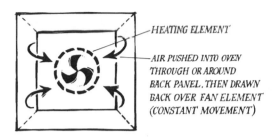

HEATING ELEMENT

AIR PUSHED INTO OVEN
THROUGH OR AROUND
BACK PANEL, THEN DRAWN
BACK OVER FAN ELEMENT
(CONSTANT MOVEMENT)

Fan assisted ovens – are they the same?

Not quite. Let me explain.

A fan assisted oven is a conventional oven with a fan at the back which circulates the heat produced in the oven. Although there is no element around the fan, many of the advantages of 'pure' fan cooking apply, with only one or two limitations.

Manufacturers of fan assisted ovens generally recommend pre-heating for a few minutes and using a maximum of two shelves at a time for batch baking, though new technology may mean that three shelves can be used on some models. Be prepared to move shelves around if even browning is required.

Fan assisted ovens are nearly always multi-function ovens and incorporate many of the cooking functions examined in the section starting on page 20.

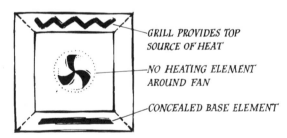

GRILL PROVIDES TOP
SOURCE OF HEAT

NO HEATING ELEMENT
AROUND FAN

CONCEALED BASE ELEMENT

Advantages of Fan Cooking at a Glance

It is important that you read the following information before you start cooking in order to appreciate fully just what a new fan oven is capable of. Many of these points will be illustrated in more detail in later chapters.

> ALWAYS READ THE INSTRUCTION BOOK
> BEFORE COOKING FOR THE FIRST TIME
> IN YOUR NEW OVEN

No preheating necessary except for certain dishes

This is because hot air begins to circulate as soon as the oven is turned on. The exceptions are yeast mixtures, scones, whisked sponges, batch baking, Yorkshire puddings, oven chips, frozen foods and dishes with contents already hot. Even then preheating is only necessary for 5–8 minutes, NOT until the thermostat light goes out. If cooking from cold, increase the cooking time by 5–10 minutes for HIGH temperature cooking.

More even cooking – perfect for batch baking and freezer cooking

Not every corner of a fan oven is at precisely the same temperature but, because of the constant flow of air, it is possible to cook on several levels at once, thus saving time and energy.

Most ovens are produced with four adjustable shelves, with a variety of runner positions, to allow most dishes to be cooked equally well on any shelf. If using four shelves for batch baking, items on the top tray may differ slightly in colour. Three shelves is the optimum number for uniform batch baking. Where possible, place dishes so that they are not directly above or below others and place them at an equal distance from the front and back: this helps to allow maximum movement of air. If you are using an oven with a filter over the fan, it can be removed for baking: this again increases the air flow.

Temperatures can be lower and cooking times can be reduced

Moving air in and around the food transfers the heat more efficiently than air heated by conduction only. As one can blow hot food to cool it, so hot air can be blown on to it to heat it more efficiently. These lower temperatures also mean that food does not spoil as quickly if left in for longer.

More economical

Preheating is not usually necessary, therefore there is no wasted cooking time, and the lower temperatures reduce the energy used.

Basting not always necessary when roasting

Joints of meat with their own fat and poultry brushed with butter or oil both seal very quickly and the air circulating around the joint keeps the meat moist and succulent. This will be explained more fully in the Roasting section (see page 25).

Food can be 'grilled' using fan heat only

This method of 'grilling' (sometimes known as thermo- or thermal grilling) is unique to fan and fan assisted ovens and will be explained fully in a section devoted to this type of cooking (see page 52).

Flavours do not transfer from one dish to another

The air is constantly moving, and in most ovens there is a filter or catalyser and venting system which allows exchange of air. Flavours do not have time to linger.

The oven stays cleaner

Fat on meat is less likely to spit and burn at lower temperatures and splashing is kept to a minimum.

The oven door can be opened during cooking without the risk of a cake sinking

Of course this should not be taken to extremes but, if opening the door to take something out or put something in, the small amount of heat lost is rapidly replaced. This means timings can be staggered as cakes can be removed or put in while others are cooking.

The automatic timer can be used efficiently and accurately

No preheating is necessary before cooking commences. When cooking several different dishes together, try to choose foods which require approximately the same temperature and time, although dishes can be 'slowed down' slightly by using larger containers and covering with aluminium foil. Also a small dish can be slowed down by placing it on a shelf immediately below a larger item on the shelf above, thus blanking off some of the circulating hot air.

Facility for defrosting

Usually by using the fan only, with no heat. This method of defrosting is particularly good for frozen cakes and desserts rather than meat. For further details see 'Defrost' in the Multi-function section (page 23).

Less checking, basting or moving of food

It is not necessary to 'watch over' the oven.

TEMPERATURES – THE KEY TO IT ALL

As already mentioned, temperatures should be reduced when cooking with forced air convection (fan). This is not because the oven becomes hotter but because the fan forces the hot air in and around the food and transfers the heat more efficiently.

Designs of ovens vary and the speed of the fan may affect temperature slightly. Remember that NO two ovens are the same, whether gas or electric, but start with the chart overleaf and adjust temperatures where necessary as you become more familiar with your oven.

Ovens which concentrate the flow of hot air through vents may require more specific positioning of trays and slightly lower temperatures may be recommended. If in doubt, refer to the manufacturer's instruction book.

As a general rule, reduce temperatures by at least 10–15° for every 100°C (a 10–15 per cent reduction). In other words the HIGHER the temperature the GREATER the reduction.

Shorten cooking time by 10 minutes for each hour ABOVE the first hour.

ALL the recipes in this book give timings for cooking in a preheated oven as well as from cold unless preheating is DEFINITELY recommended.

Temperature Chart

	Gas mark	Conventional Oven		Fan oven
very cool	1/4	200°F	100°C	90°C
	1/4	225°F	110°C	100°C
	1/2	250°F	130°C	110°C
cool	1	275°F	140°C	120–130°C
	2	300°F	150°C	130–140°C
warm	3	325°F	160°C	140–150°C
moderate	4	350°F	180°C	160°C
	5	375°F	190°C	170°C
mod. hot	6	400°F	200°C	180°C
hot	7	425°F	220°C	190–200°C
very hot	8	450°F	230°C	200–210°C
	9	475°F	240°C	210°C
	9+	500°F	250°C	220°C

Table of Cooking Temperatures for Commonly Used Items

Food	Temperature
Bread	200–210°C
Cakes:	
Creamed cake mixtures (Victoria sandwich)	160–170°C
Individual	160–170°C
Rich fruit cakes	130–140°C
Sponge sandwich (fatless)	170–180°C
Whisked sponges (Swiss (jelly) roll)	180–190°C
Casseroles	150–160°C
Complete meals	170–180°C
Fruit pies	170–180°C
General mixed cooking	160–170°C
Individual Yorkshire puddings	190–220°C
Meringues	80–100°C
Plate-warming	50–80°C
Puff pastry	190–200°C
Roasting	160–180°C
Scones	190–200°C

Automatic Cooking

Most ovens have the facility to programme the clock so that the oven will turn itself on and off in your absence. This function is particularly suited to fan cooking because the fan begins to circulate heat as soon as the oven switches itself on without a lengthy preheating time.

Tips for automatic cooking

- Choose foods which can cook for the same length of time and at approximately the same temperature.
- Dishes that require a slightly lower temperature or less time can be covered with foil or placed under a larger item on the shelf above.
- Vegetables can be cut smaller or larger to reduce or increase the required cooking time.
- Set the 'end of cooking' time to coincide with your return home or just after. This ensures that the food will not need reheating before serving.
- Food left in the oven for automatic cooking should remain as cold as possible until heating commences and needless to say the oven should be completely cold when the food is put in.
- All the ingredients of casseroles must be cold before placing in the oven.
- Frozen meat and poultry should be thoroughly defrosted.
- When the weather is warm the 'delay start' period should be kept to a minimum.
- Par-boil potatoes for roasting, and coat well in oil or melted fat to prevent discolouration.

CONVENIENCE
FOODS

Ready-prepared foods and complete meals

Convenience foods, in all forms, play a very large part in our lives but when it comes to fresh or frozen ready-to-heat meals and convenience foods instructions for heating these in fan ovens are often vague or non-existent.

Marks & Spencer, Waitrose and Safeway kindly took the time to talk to me about this and provided samples for me to test in both fan and conventional ovens. They, along with Sainsburys, also helped me to compile a list of guidelines which can be applied to all types of food, whether fresh or frozen.

Without exception, the dishes tested became hotter more quickly when heated in a fan system of cooking, even when the recommended temperature for conventional cooking was reduced by 20°C. The meals tested are included in the following chart:

Chart of Tested Ready-prepared Meals

Dish	Conventional oven (preheated for 10–15 minutes)		Fan system oven (preheated for 5 minutes)	
	Temp	*Time*	*Temp*	*Time*
MARKS AND SPENCER				
Beefsteak pie	180°C	20 minutes	160°C	20 minutes
Cannelloni (remove sleeve)	200°C	20 minutes	180°C	20 minutes
Chicken and red wine casserole	190°C	1 hour, 10 minutes	170°C	1 hour, 10 minutes
Chicken tikka masala (pierce film)	180°C	20 minutes	160°C	20 minutes
Haddock mornay (remove lid)	200°C	25 minutes	180°C	25 minutes
Lasagne (remove lid)	200°C	25 minutes	180°C	25 minutes
Sweet and sour chicken	190°C	8 minutes + 8 minutes	170°C	8 minutes + 8 minutes
Tagliatelle with ham and mushrooms	180°C	25 minutes	160°C	25 minutes
Tarte aux cerises	180°C	15 minutes	160°C	15 minutes
Vegetable bake	190°C	30 minutes	170°C	30 minutes

Dish	Conventional oven (preheated for 10–15 minutes)		Fan system oven (preheated for 5 minutes)	
	Temp	Time	Temp	Time
WAITROSE				
Bombay potatoes	180°C	30 minutes	160°C	30 minutes
Cauliflower cheese (remove lid)	180°C	40 minutes	160°C	30 minutes
Chicken in black bean sauce	180°C	25 minutes	160°C	25 minutes
Chicken korma	180°C	30 minutes	160°C	30 minutes
Crispy seaweed	190°C	3 minutes	170°C	3 minutes
Lasagne (remove lid)	180°C	30 minutes	160°C	30 minutes
Moussaka (remove lid)	200°C	35–40 minutes	180°C	35–40 minutes
Pilau rice	180°C	20 minutes	160°C	20 minutes
Salmon and broccoli pie	180°C	30 minutes	160°C	30 minutes
Shepherd's pie (remove lid)	180°C	30 minutes	160°C	30 minutes
Singapore noodles	180°C	20 minutes	160°C	20 minutes
Sweet and sour pork (peel back lid)	180°C	15-20 minutes	160°C	15–20 minutes
Tagliatelle carbonara	200°C	20 minutes	180°C	20 minutes
Tagliatelle niçoise (remove lid)	200°C	30 minutes	180°C	30 minutes

Dish	Conventional oven (preheated for 10–15 minutes)		Fan system oven (preheated for 5 minutes)	
	Temp	Time	Temp	Time
SAFEWAY				
Cannelloni (pierce lid)	190°C	20 minutes	170°C	20 minutes
Chicken and mushroom pie	190°C	25 minutes	170°C	25 minutes
Chinese style chicken with egg fried rice (pierce lid twice)	190°C	20 minutes	170°C	20 minutes
Cumberland pie (remove film)	200°C	25–30 minutes	180°C	25–30 minutes
Farmhouse lattice-topped pie	190°C	25 minutes	170°C	25 minutes
Lasagne (remove lid)	190°C	25 minutes	170°C	25 minutes
Liver and bacon (pierce lid)	200°C	25 minutes	180°C	25 minutes
Spaghetti bolognese (pierce lid)	190°C	20 minutes	170°C	20 minutes

A guide to cooking frozen and fresh ready-prepared meals and convenience foods by the fan system.

• Read the cooking instructions on the packet and use a solid baking sheet if one is recommended. Always remember that using higher temperatures than suggested may damage a non-foil container.

• Preheat your oven for 5–8 minutes **or** increase the recommended cooking time by at least 5 minutes.

• Always preheat the oven for frozen foods which have to be cooked from frozen.

• Lower the recommended temperature given for conventional ovens by 10°C for every 100°C (refer to temperature chart on page 12), e.g. oven chips reduce from 220°C to 190–200°C.

• If temperatures have been reduced, the timings should remain the same as for conventional cooking unless the cooking time is LONGER than one hour, in which case reduce the time by 10 minutes for every hour ABOVE the first hour.

• If using only ONE shelf of food, always position it near the centre of the oven.

• If cooking more than two shelves of food, you may need to increase the recommended cooking time by 10–15 minutes.

• Always use your judgement to ensure that cook/chill foods are reheated until piping hot throughout.

• Never reheat cook/chill or ready-prepared frozen meals more than once as they have nearly always been partly cooked during their manufacture.

MULTI-FUNCTION OVENS

Although all the recipes in this book relate to cooking in the fan system, you may have some, or all, of the following functions on your oven if it is a multi-function oven.

Because of the possibility of a concealed element in the base of the oven NEVER place food or dishes on the base of your oven unless the manufacturer suggests it.

ALWAYS refer to your manufacturer's instruction manual for guidance on the use of all the following additional functions.

Cooling fan
Please note that even if you are using a conventional function that does not use the hot air fan you may still hear a fan working. This is the cooling fan and it can work even when the oven control is in the 'off' position if there is residual heat in the oven. This fan does not perform a cooking function. Some ovens without a cooling fan suggest turning the oven on to 'fan only' to cool the oven more quickly.

Conventional system (traditional cooking, natural convection etc.)
In most fan ovens with a conventional cooking system the heat sources are a concealed element in the base of the oven and the outer ring of the exposed grill element at the top of the oven.

The oven must be preheated for 10–15 minutes. The heat will naturally rise to the top of the oven and therefore the bottom of the oven will be cooler. Use only one shelf unless cooking an additional dish needing a lower temperature in the base. The middle shelf position gives the best heat distribution.

The conventional method can be used for casseroles, fruit cakes and recipes with a high egg content. It will give darker surface browning on pastry dishes than the fan system.

Full top heat and low base

Preheat and use for *au gratin* dishes and casseroles to brown on top while keeping the food underneath hot.

Base heat only

The concealed base element comes on usually at full power and can be used for finishing off and crisping up or drying out pastry and pizza bases. This is excellent for drying out the pastry underneath a *bœuf en croûte*. In some ovens the base element is regulated at a low temperature for proving of bread and pizza dough. Base heat may or may not be controlled by the thermostat.

Preheat unless the dish is already in the oven, in which case use for the last 15 minutes of cooking.

Low top heat and full base heat

This is a form of conventional cooking where the top heat has been reduced to balance out the distribution of heat in the oven. The source of the top heat is usually the outer edge of the grill element.

This method can be used for rich fruit cakes which have a tendency to over-brown on top. It can also be used on a low setting for proving bread and for delicate baked foods, meringues or tin loaves.

Overall temperature is controlled by the thermostat.

Fan cooking with additional base heat

The base element operates in conjunction with the heat distributed by the fan element to give direct heat from the floor of the oven. Some ovens offer this as a pizza- or bread-baking system as the extra heat helps to give a very crisp base. This system is also used for quiches or pies with a very moist filling to ensure that the pastry cooks underneath without the need for blind baking.

Preheat the oven for 5–8 minutes before placing the dish on the shelf nearest to the bottom heat. The element gives off a pre-set level of its power while the heat from the fan is regulated by the thermostat. This means that other food can be cooked simultaneously in the rest of the oven.

If the oven is fan assisted, the base heat will be distributed by the fan only. Therefore it is recommended that only one shelf be used because the base element is the only one operating.

Top heat in conjunction with fan

This can be used for cooking dishes which require different temperatures in the oven at the same time. The top of the oven is approximately 30 per cent hotter than the base.

Preheat and, if food on the top is to be cooked for a long time, cover for the first part of cooking to prevent over-browning.

Top heat only

The top heat source comes on, usually at full power (not as hot as the grill). It gives a more diffused heat than the normal grill element and can be used for dishes with a meringue topping where only the meringue needs to cook, and for finishing off cheese, potato or pastry toppings. The heat may or may not be controlled by the thermostat.

Preheat for 5–8 minutes before use, unless food is already in the oven.

Top and bottom elements working in conjunction with normal fan system

This is generally used as an intensive baking or 'multi-bake' system, the majority of the heat coming from the base of the oven. The main advantage is that dishes such as quiches and fruit pies can be cooked without the need to blind bake the pastry, providing only the shelf level nearest the base of the oven is used.

If the oven is preheated, two shelves of food can be cooked together.

Temperatures selected should be the same as for normal fan cooking.

This system is also incorporated on some ovens as part of the pre-heating process. It helps reduce the pre-heating time, especially when higher temperatures are required.

Defrost

This function may have its own symbol on the control panel or the existing fan setting would be used. In general the fan works without any heat and circulates room-temperature air inside the oven, which reduces the defrosting time of frozen foods by about one-third. In some ovens a low temperature of between 30°C and 50°C may operate.

This method of defrosting is particularly good for frozen desserts and cakes but is less suitable for poultry, meat and fish. Quiches, pastries, biscuits, scones, bread, doughnuts, buns, croissants, cakes coated with icing or chocolate, cheesecakes etc. can also be defrosted in this way.

It is best to thaw fish, meat or poultry slowly in the refrigerator whenever possible. However this process can be accelerated by thawing in the fan oven. Small pieces or thin slices of frozen fish or meat items such as fish fillets, frozen peeled prawns, cubed or minced meat, and thin chops will be defrosted in 1–2 hours.

- Cover food or leave in the bag to prevent drying out while defrosting.

- Place food in a single layer and turn over half-way through.

- If food is to be cooked, always defrost thoroughly and cook immediately after defrosting.

- Store desserts in the refrigerator after defrosting.

- All trays and racks must be thoroughly washed after use.

Pizza or baking stone

Some ovens offer the facility to use a proper baking stone for cooking pizza, naan bread, flat breads etc. It sometimes comes with the oven but is more often available as an optional extra. The pizza stone is heated by means of an element which plugs into the base of the oven.

It generally needs preheating for 30–40 minutes on a high setting or full power before cooking commences. Once hot it will retain its heat for some time, therefore the temperature can be reduced.

ROASTING

Meat

The swift movement of hot air seals the meat quickly, keeping in the flavours, juices and nutrients, resulting in a roast that is almost self-basting, and shrinks less than a traditional roast.

Very lean joints may need basting, and poultry should be brushed over the breast with a little oil or melted butter.

For best results place the meat to be roasted on a grid, above the deep roasting tin supplied with your oven. This allows maximum movement of air around the meat. Some ovens provide an anti-splash trivet; place the meat on it or on a grid above.

Roasting bags or foil can be used to cover the meat but you will be losing the benefits of 'open roasting' in your fan oven.

If preferred, it is, of course, still possible to roast in a more traditional way, with the roast sitting in the base of the tin and the potatoes and vegetables around it, but this does restrict the air flow around the meat.

Resting

All meat will carve better if allowed to rest, loosely covered in foil, for 15 minutes. This allows the opportunity for finishing the potatoes at a higher temperature and for cooking the Yorkshire puddings. (See the recipe for Roast Beef and Yorkshire Pudding on page 44 for more details.)

Water in the roasting tin?

Some manufacturers recommend placing a good half pint of water or stock in the base of the roasting tin when roasting. This also helps to reduce the splashing and retains juices to add to the gravy. Your oven must have a good venting or filtering system to prevent a build-up of steam in the oven, although a little steam causes no harm and quickly disperses when the door is opened. If the liquid evaporates it can be topped up during cooking with HOT water.

Roasting potatoes

If open roasting, as recommended, the potatoes can be cooked either in a separate tin tossed in oil or fat or in the roasting tin under the meat, providing the grid can be positioned one level higher than the tin to allow room for the potatoes. They will not need basting but can be turned once half-way through cooking.

Another popular method is a form of dry roasting. Par-boil the potatoes for 3 minutes and toss in vegetable oil, making sure they are completely coated to prevent discolouration. Sprinkle with a little salt. Place them on the grid around the joint and open roast them for one hour. They will not need turning or basting and the end result will be crisp, brown and with a lower fat content.

Timings and temperatures

The following temperatures will cook poultry and meat without excessive spitting but if possible start off at a higher temperature of 190–200°C for the first 15–20 minutes to seal and crisp the food. Some ovens offer this as an 'auto roast' system which boosts up the temperature initially then reduces it to the pre-set temperature for cooking through.

Timings are based on an oven preheated for 5–8 minutes. If placing in a cold oven, add an extra 10 minutes to the total time.

Guide to Open Roasting Meat and Poultry

Higher temperatures can be used for very lean meat (fillet or tenderloin)

Roast	Time per 450g/1 lb	Temperature
Beef: topside, top rump sirloin off the bone, rib	20, + 20 minutes (medium)	160–180°C
roast on the bone	15, + 15 minutes (rare)	160–180°C
Chicken	20–25, + 20 minutes	160–170°C
Duck (prick the skin)	20–25, + 20 minutes	180–190°C
Goose	20–25, + 20 minutes	170–180°C
Ham (boil for half the total cooking time)	25, + 25 minutes	160–170°C
Lamb	25–30, + 25 minutes	160–170°C
Pheasant	50–60 minutes total	170–180°C
Pork	first 20 minutes	200°C
	30–35, + 30 minutes	160–170°C
Turkey: up to 5.5 kg/12 lb	20, + 20 minutes	150–160°C
over 5.5 kg/12 lb	15, + 15 minutes	150–160°C
Veal	25–30, + 25 minutes	160–170°C

COOK'S NOTES

All meat should be at room temperature when it is put in the oven. Don't forget to add the weight of any stuffing before calculating the cooking time.
If you prefer to cover the joint, or like your meat really well cooked, increase the cooking times slightly as necessary.

Temperature probes

Many fan ovens now come with a temperature probe. This is a thermometer which tells you the internal temperature of your food during cooking. It is mainly used when roasting joints but can be used in terrines and pâtés, and when reheating pies and casseroles. The probe allows you to pre-set the required internal temperature of the food. Once this is reached, the oven will usually turn itself off. Any oven temperature can be used and any method of cooking except grilling, which would damage the probe.

The TIP of the probe registers the internal temperature of the meat/food being cooked, therefore the tip must be positioned in the thickest part of the meat and not touching a bone as this will give the wrong reading. (Bone conducts heat quicker than meat.)

With poultry, which has a lot of bones, it is a good idea to put the probe between the leg and breast or to push the probe through the rib cage and into the centre of a large onion placed in the cavity or into the stuffing. It is still advisable to test poultry in the traditional way by checking that the juices run clear when a fork is inserted between the leg and the breast.

Roasting with the temperature probe

Roughly calculate the cooking time by weight to enable you to plan the rest of the meal but be prepared for it to be ready a little earlier than estimated.

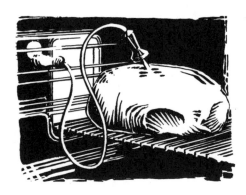

Position the meat on the roasting grid as for normal roasting. Insert the sharp tip of the probe into the centre of the thickest part of the meat.

Programme the temperature according to your manufacturer's instruction manual. The probe stays in until the meat is cooked. Once the selected internal temperature selected has been reached the oven gives an audible signal and turns off. Some ovens even give an early warning when the temperature is within 5° of the temperature selected. This allows time to give finishing touches to other food being served.

Remove the meat immediately and allow to rest, wrapped in foil, before carving. The internal temperature may rise 5–10° while resting. Allow for this in your calculations.

Do not leave meat in the oven or it may over-cook. Wipe the probe clean – NEVER put it in the dishwasher.

Suggested temperatures

Obviously tastes vary so these can only be guidelines, especially for beef. Try them first then adjust to find your ideal temperatures.

Food		Temperature
Beef:	blue – rare	40–45°C
	rare	45–55°C
	medium	55–65°C
	well done	70–80°C
Chicken:	well done (probe in onion)	85°C
Ham:	well done	84°C
Lamb:	pink	70–75°C
	medium – well done	80–85°C
Pork:	well done	85°C
Terrines and pâtés:	83°C	
Turkey:	well done	85°C

Grilling

Every single fan oven has a radiant element in its roof to be used for traditional grilling. In the case of a double oven you may have two grills, or just one, in the second oven.

Always check your manufacturer's instructions on the operation of this grill. Some ovens grill with the door open, others with the door closed. If your oven offers a choice, in general grilling is better with the door closed to prevent smoke and fumes coming into the kitchen. However, if a really hot grill is required (e.g. for a brûlée or thin cuts of meat), an open door will boost the grill temperature. Some manufacturers class this as 'barbecue grilling'.

Some ovens offer the option of a half grill as well as a full grill. If your oven has a fat filter, this must be in place for roasting and grilling.

Tips for grilling

- To prevent drying out I would always recommend preheating the grill on the required setting for 5–8 minutes and adding salt only after grilling.
- Place food on a metal grid wherever possible to allow maximum circulation of heat and to lift the food away from the fat. Some ovens include a trivet to be used underneath the grid to reduce spitting.
- Do not place the food too close to the element. Grilling will be more even if food is at least 6–8 cm (3–4 in) away from the element.
- Dry meat or fish with kitchen paper before grilling, and brush lean meats and fish with a little oil or melted butter.
- Mushrooms and tomatoes can be placed underneath the grid when grilling meats.
- For toast or rare steaks, preheat the grill on full power then reduce as necessary.

Fan assisted grilling

On a multi-function oven this system offers an alternative method of grilling food.

The fan 'assists' the conventional grill element by circulating the heat around and underneath the food being cooked, thus reducing the need for turning. It will operate in one of two ways:

A. The top element is the source of heat and in addition the fan works continuously throughout the grilling (with no heat coming from the fan) to circulate this heat around the food.

B. The grill element and the fan element work alternately throughout the cooking process.

Confusion arises because there are different terms to describe this method of cooking, such as hot air grilling and thermal grilling. DO NOT confuse fan assisted grilling with the method of hot air grilling which does not use a radiant element at all.

Fan assisted grilling is recommended for all meat and fish grilling. The oven door is usually closed for this setting and therefore cooking smells are reduced. The end result is extremely succulent as the fan helps to seal in the juices and flavour of the food.

Tips for fan assisted grilling

• To obtain equal browning on both sides turn the food once. Flat fish can be placed on a solid baking sheet and should not need turning.

• Bacon placed on a grid does not curl up and will cook beautifully without turning.

If your oven has this system of cooking you will find that you need your conventional grill only for cooking rare steaks, toast, cheese on toast, brûlées or crumpets or when only surface browning is required.

General Cooking Guide for Grilling

Adjust according to the thickness of the food and whether it is to be rare, medium or well done.

Cooking times for fan assisted grilling may be 2–5 minutes shorter

Food		Total time
Bacon		8–12 minutes
Cheese on toast		3–5 minutes
Chicken breasts		20–25 minutes
Chicken joints		30–40 minutes
Fish fillets		8–10 minutes
Fish (whole)		15–20 minutes
Gammon steaks		10–12 minutes
Hamburgers		15–20 minutes
Kebabs		20–25 minutes
Lamb chops		20–25 minutes
Liver		12–15 minutes
Pork chops		20–30 minutes
Sausages (large)		15–20 minutes
Steaks	rare	4–6 minutes each side
	medium	6–8 minutes each side
	well done	10–12 minutes each side

Fan assisted grilling as a roasting system

Once again different manufacturers call this by different names, such as circo-roasting, turbo-grilling, roastamatic, rotitherm, ventilated grilling etc. The basic principle is the same.

When this method is used for roasting joints of meat and poultry the end result is similar to rotisserie cooked food. It takes slightly less time than normal roasting and produces a crisp finish.

The joint must be turned once if an all-round crispness is required but in general turning is not necessary.

Tips for fan assisted grilling as a roasting system

- Suitable for poultry or joints up to 5.5 kg (12 lb).
- Position the meat on a metal grid in the lower half of the oven with a drip tray underneath. This allows hot air from the grill to circulate freely around the oven. If planning to turn poultry, start it breast-side down.
- Always cook a joint with the fat-side uppermost in order to crisp it.
- A temperature of 200–225°C will give a barbecue finish and should be used only for lean meat that does not require long to cook. Lower temperatures of 165–200°C will give a more traditional finish and will ensure that crackling on pork is lovely and crisp without excessive spitting and soiling of the oven. In general, I find it better to use the lower temperature for fattier meat.
- Cooking by this method is a little quicker but so much depends on the temperature selected and the thickness of the joint, I would suggest using the timings in the roasting chart given for fan oven roasting to begin with and allow 10–15 minutes standing time (see page 27). If your oven comes with a temperature probe, check with your instruction manual whether it can be used on this system.
- Your oven manufacturer may suggest putting water in the drip tray to cover the base as for normal roasting. This also reduces the spitting and gives some juices to add to the gravy or sauce.

Rotisserie cooking

Although the fan system itself produces excellent roasts, many ovens provide a rotisserie, which will give the flavour and finish of barbecue-cooked food. Always use it with a grill function to obtain the best flavour. Preheating is not required. Secure the food on to the spit firmly, so that bits do not fall away. Ensure that the spit can move freely. Use the roasting tin underneath to catch the drips.

The finished result will vary depending on the temperature selected. Higher temperatures will produce a darker barbecue finish.

Refer to your manufacturer's handbook for instructions on how to operate.

ROAST CHICKEN WITH ONION

SERVES 4–6

※

---

1 roasting chicken (weight as required)
1 Spanish onion, halved and sliced
50 g/2 oz/^{1}/$_4$ cup butter, softened
Salt and freshly ground black pepper

---

1. Wipe the chicken and pull out any loose fat from inside the cavity. Push your fingers gently under the skin from the wishbone end and loosen as much of the skin over the breast as possible, trying not to break it.

2. Push slices of onion one at a time under the skin as far as they will go. Cover as much of the breast as possible with onion.

3. Spread the softened butter over the breast and season. Place on a grid above a roasting tin and roast.

TEMP	TIME
160-170°C (no need to preheat)	20–25 minutes per 450 g/1 lb plus 20 minutes
COOK'S NOTE	
Cook breast-side down for the first 20–30 minutes then turn over.	

Alternative cooking function if available (refer to your manufacturer's instructions first):

Suggested temp: 170–180°C or equivalent
Time: 20–25 minutes per 450 g/1 lb

ROAST GOOSE WITH DATE AND APPLE STUFFING

SERVES 6–8

✳

4 kg/9 lb approx. fresh goose (giblets removed)
1 packet sage and onion stuffing
1 large cooking (tart) apple
100 g/4 oz/²⁄₃ cup dates, chopped
Freshly ground black pepper
Butter, melted

1 Prepare the stuffing according to the instructions on the packet and allow to cool. Peel, core and chop the apple, then add it to the mix with the dates.

2 Wipe out the goose cavity, remove the wishbone for easier carving.

3 Stuff the cavity and secure the opening with a small skewer or cocktail stick.

4 Place the goose on a grid above a roasting tin. Prick the skin gently with a fork without piercing the meat. Brush the melted butter over the breast and season with pepper. Roast.

TEMP	TIME
170°C (no need to preheat)	25 minutes per 450 g/1 lb plus 25 minutes (preheated) OR 25 minutes per 450 g/1 lb plus 35 minutes (from cold)
COOK'S NOTE	
For extra crispness preheat the oven for 8 minutes at 190–200°C and cook for 20 minutes before reducing to 170°C.	

STUFFED ROAST DUCK WITH APPLE AND ONION SAUCE

SERVES 4–6

✳

1.75–2.25 kg/4–5 lb fresh duckling
1 packet sage and onion stuffing

For the sauce:
2 large onions
2 cooking (tart) apples
25 g/1 oz/^{1}/$_8$ cup butter
25 g/1 oz/^{1}/$_8$ cup sugar
Salt

1 Prepare the stuffing according to the instructions.

2 Wipe the duck. Stuff the cavity and secure with skewers. Weigh with the stuffing.

3 Place on a wire rack above a roasting tin. Roast, draining off some of the fat during cooking if necessary.

4 After 30 minutes of cooking prick the skin gently (not too deep) with a fine skewer to allow surplus fat to run out.

5 Meanwhile prepare the sauce. Peel and slice the onions and apples.

6 Melt the butter in a pan and add onions, apples, sugar and salt.

7 Cover the pan and simmer gently until the onions and apples are tender. Turn the mixture into a serving bowl and serve hot.

TEMP	TIME
180–190°C (no need to preheat)	20–25 minutes per 450g/1 lb
COOK'S NOTE	
The sauce can be made in advance and reheated in a microwave.	

Additional cooking function if available (refer to your manufacturer's instructions for guidance):

Suggested temp: 170–180°C or equivalent
Time: for the last 20 minutes of cooking

ROAST TURKEY

✳

Every year I seem to find another method of cooking a turkey. It matters not which method you choose – whether wrapped in buttered muslin, covered in a tent of foil, turned upside-down, placed on its side, or simply roasted and basted as one would a chicken.

Whatever your favourite method just remember the golden rules of fan cooking and reduce the temperature and time accordingly.

The following method is one I personally find successful and I hope you will too.

---

1 oven-ready turkey (weight as required)
75 g/3 oz/¹/₃ cup butter, softened
450–700 g/1–1.5 lb stuffing
Freshly ground black pepper

---

1 Remove wishbone for easier carving, if preferred.

2 Push your fingers under the skin of the breast and loosen it from the flesh.

3 Spread 50 g/2 oz/¹/₄ cup butter between the skin and the breast.

4 Stuff the neck end of the bird, pull the skin flap firmly over the stuffing and secure with a small skewer or cocktail stick.

5 Spread the rest of the butter over the breast, legs and wings and season with black pepper.

6 Do not truss the bird; this will allow maximum exposure to the heat.

7 Place the turkey on the grid or trivet supplied with your oven and position in the oven on the bottom runner. Roast.

8 Have a large piece of foil ready. Lift the tray out of the oven, place the bird on the foil (if possible upside-down). Cover with the foil and rest for at least 30 minutes. This allows time to crisp up the potatoes, cook the parsnips, bacon rolls, etc.

TEMP	TIME
150-160°C (no need to preheat)	Up to 6.5 kg/14 lbs – 20 minutes per 450 g/1 lb plus 20 minutes Over 6.5 kg/14 lbs – 15 minutes per 450 g/1 lb plus 15 minutes (see chart on page 27)

COOK'S NOTES
If the turkey is covered with foil the cooking time will be longer. A small turkey can be cooked on its side or breast-side down but a larger bird will be difficult to manoeuvre and turn from side to side during cooking.

SHOULDER OF LAMB WITH APRICOT STUFFING

SERVES 4

✳

1 shoulder of lamb, boned
1 small onion, finely chopped
15 g/^{1}/$_2$ oz/1 tbsp butter
1 × 425 g/15 oz can apricot halves, drained
25 g/1 oz/^{1}/$_2$ cup fresh white breadcrumbs
5 ml/1 tsp chopped mint (fresh OR dried)
5 ml/1 tsp chopped fresh parsley
Pinch of dried thyme
Pinch of ground cinnamon
Salt and freshly ground black pepper

1 Remove any tough skin from the meat and spread out flat.

2 Cook the onion in the butter until tender. Chop seven apricot halves and combine with the onions, breadcrumbs, herbs, cinnamon and seasoning in a basin.

3 Spread the mixture inside the lamb and roll. Tie with four pieces of string.

4 Weigh the meat. Place on a grid or trivet above a roasting tin and roast.

5 For the last 10 minutes place the remaining apricot halves on the grid.

6 Allow the joint to rest for 15 minutes loosely wrapped in foil, then slice thickly and garnish with the apricot halves.

TEMP	TIME
160–170°C (no need to preheat)	25 minutes per 450 g/1 lb plus 25 minutes
COOK'S NOTES	
There is no need to bone the joint yourself; ask your butcher to do it or buy one ready-prepared from the supermarket. Some of the apricot juice can be used to flavour the gravy.	

Alternative cooking function if available (refer to your manufacturer's instructions for guidance)

Suggested temp: 160–170°C or equivalent
Time: as in recipe above

FRENCH ROAST RACKS OF LAMB WITH ROSEMARY AND GARLIC

COURTESY OF NEFF (UK) LTD

SERVES 6–8

✳

3 best end necks of lamb, chined
3 garlic cloves, skinned and crushed
60 ml/4 tbsp wholegrain mustard
30 ml/2 tbsp olive oil
30 ml/2 tbsp chopped fresh rosemary
OR 5 ml/1 tsp dried rosemary
90 ml/6 tbsp fresh white breadcrumbs
Salt and freshly ground black pepper

1 With a sharp pointed knife, trim the fat off the ends of the cutlets to expose about 5 cm/2 in of bone. Place the racks, fat side up, on a grid above a roasting tin.

2 Mix the garlic, mustard, oil, rosemary, breadcrumbs, salt and pepper together in a small basin. Spread this mixture over the lamb to cover the fat evenly. Roast.

3 Leave to stand loosely covered for 10–15 minutes, then carve into individual cutlets.

TEMP	TIME
160–170°C (from cold)	35–40 minutes (medium) 45–50 minutes (well done)

COOK'S NOTE
If your oven has a meat thermometer use this and refer to the chart on page 29 for suggested temperatures.

ROAST LEG OF LAMB WITH ROSEMARY

SERVES 6–8

✳

1 leg of lamb

50 g/2 oz/¹/₄ cup butter

Salt and freshly ground black pepper

Leaves from few sprigs of rosemary

1 garlic clove, cut into slivers

1 Spread the butter over the lamb and season well. Press the rosemary leaves into the butter.

2 Make a few slits in the lamb and insert slivers of garlic.

3 Place the joint on a rack above a roasting tin and roast.

TEMP	TIME
160–170°C (no need to preheat)	25–30 minutes per 450 g/1 lb plus 25 minutes

ROAST BEEF AND YORKSHIRE PUDDING

✳

1 joint of topside, top rump or sirloin

Freshly ground black pepper

1 Weigh beef and calculate cooking time by the roasting chart.

2 Place on a grid, season with pepper and roast.

TEMP	TIME
170–180°C (first 15 minutes can be 200°C or above)	20 minutes per 450 g/1 lb plus 20 minutes (medium) 15 minutes per 450 g/1 lb plus 15 minutes (rare)

YORKSHIRE PUDDING MIX

SERVES 6–8

175 g/6 oz/1¹/₂ cups plain (all-purpose) flour

Good pinch of salt

2 eggs

275 ml/¹/₂ pint/1¹/₄ cups milk OR milk and water mixed

25 g/1 oz/2 tbsp lard

Sift

1 Sieve the flour and salt into a mixing bowl and make a well in the centre.

2 Crack the eggs into the well and beat gently with a mixer. Add the liquid a little at a time beating well between each addition.

3 Allow the batter to stand for several hours is possible. Before use add 2 tablespoons cold water and beat in for a few seconds.

4 Raise the temperature of the oven to 190–220°C. Using 1 tray of *muffin tins* individual pudding or small cake tins, OR 2 round pudding tins approx. 18 cm (7 in) diameter, OR 1 large rectangular tin, put a knife point of lard into each section of an individual pudding tin (about 15 g/^{1}/$_2$ oz/1 tbsp into each round tin or 25 g/1 oz/2 tbsp into a large tin) and put into the oven until the fat becomes very hot (hazy).

5 Half-fill each tin with batter (it should sizzle) and bake until well risen and golden brown. If using large tins the puddings may take a little longer to cook.

400° - 425°

TEMP	TIME
190–220°C (already hot)	20–30 minutes

COOK'S NOTE
Remove the beef from the oven before putting in the trays and wrap well in foil to rest. If you do this, bear in mind that the centre of the beef will rise a little in temperature so allow for this in your cooking calculations.

Will make a little dip in top of pudding while it is cooking - Pour gravy over the yorkshire Pudding.

ROAST FILLET OF BEEF

SERVES 4–6

✳

900 g–1.5 kg/2–3 lb fillet of beef, trimmed of fat
2–3 garlic cloves
Olive oil
Ground black pepper

1 Peel garlic and cut into slivers. Make small slits in the beef at irregular intervals and insert the garlic. Brush the fillet with oil and season with ground black pepper.

2 Place the beef on a roasting grid and roast for 45 minutes–1 hour depending on how well done you like it (see chart on page 29)

TEMP	TIME
190–220°C) (preheated for 8 minutes)	45 minutes – 1 hour

TRADITIONAL ROAST PORK

SERVES 4

✳

900 g/1.5 kg/2–3 lb boneless pork leg joint, rind well scored
Oil, for brushing
5–10 ml/1–2 tsp salt

1 Score the rind well. Dry the joint and brush the rind with oil then rub with a little salt.

2 Place the joint, uncovered, on a metal grid or trivet above a roasting tin and cook. There is no need to baste during cooking. Allow to rest for 15 minutes prior to carving.

TEMP	TIME
160–170°C (no need to preheat)	30 minutes per 450 g/1 lb plus 30 minutes
COOK'S NOTE	
Serve with apple sauce or apple slices cooked on a tray for 20 minutes.	

NB: Increase the temperature to 190–200°C for the first 30 minutes to crisp the crackling.

Alternative cooking function if available (refer to your manufacturer's instructions for guidance):

Suggested temp: 170–180°C or equivalent
Time: for the last 20 minutes to crisp the crackling

This function can also be used throughout the cooking time but the joint may need turning

Suggested temp: 160–170°C or equivalent
Time: 30 minutes per 450 g/1 lb plus 30 minutes

STUFFED LOIN OF PORK

SERVES 6

❋

1.5–1.75 kg/3–4 lb boned loin of pork
Oil, for brushing
Salt

For the stuffing:
50 g/2 oz/¹/₄ cup butter
1 onion, chopped
100 g/4 oz/2 cups fresh breadcrumbs
5 ml/1 tsp dried sage
10 ml/2 tsp chopped fresh parsley
1 cooking (tart) apple, peeled, cored and chopped
Salt and freshly ground black pepper
1 egg, beaten

1 Gently fry the onion in the butter until soft. Add all the other stuffing ingredients and mix well.

2 Trim any surplus fat from the pork and score the skin. Lay skin-side down on a board and spread the stuffing on top. If necessary cut a pocket into the flesh near the skin to take more of the stuffing.

3 Roll up the joint. Tie with string at 2.5 cm (1 in) intervals and weigh. If the loin cannot be rolled tight enough to hold in the stuffing, place it skin-side up on a piece of greaseproof paper the same size as the joint to prevent the stuffing falling through the grid.

4 Brush the skin with a little oil and sprinkle salt over it.

TEMP	TIME
160–170°C (preheat for 8 minutes)	30–35 minutes per 450 g/1 lb plus 30 minutes

COOK'S NOTE
Increase the temperature to 190–200°C for the first 30 minutes to crisp the skin.

Alternative cooking function if available (refer to your manufacturer's instructions for guidance):

Suggested temp: 170–180°C or equivalent
Time: for the last 15–20 minutes of cooking to produce superb crackling

HONEY-GLAZED GAMMON

SERVES 6–8

✳

1.5–1.75 kg/3–4 lb gammon piece
1 bay leaf
1 onion, quartered
6–8 juniper berries OR peppercorns
30 ml/2 tbsp clear honey
30 ml/2 tbsp soft brown OR demerara (light brown) sugar
5 ml/1 tsp mustard powder
5 ml/1 tsp ground ginger OR cinnamon

1 Allow 20–25 minutes per 450 g/1 lb plus 20 minutes, to calculate the total cooking time. Cover with water and soak for at least 3 hours or overnight. Rinse well then cover with more cold water in a large pan. Add the bay leaf, onion and juniper berries or peppercorns. Bring slowly to the boil, skim off any scum, reduce heat, cover with a lid and cook for half the total cooking time.

2 Drain the joint and remove skin while still warm with a sharp knife. Score the fat with diagonal cuts across the fat to form diamond shapes. Be careful not to cut into the meat.

3 Mix the honey, sugar, mustard powder and ginger or cinnamon together and spoon over the top of the joint.

4 Place the joint on a metal grid above the drip tray.

5 Bake, basting occasionally with the juices in the pan. Raise the temperature for the last 20 minutes of cooking time.

TEMP	TIME
160°C (no need to preheat) 190–200°C for last 20 minutes	10–12 minutes per 450 g/1 lb plus 20 minutes in oven

Alternative cooking method if available (refer to your manufacturer's instructions first):

Suggested temp: 180–190°C or equivalent
Time: for the last 20 minutes of cooking

HOT AIR GRILLING

This system uses the fan element only; some manufacturers call this thermo- or thermal grilling.

It is a method of cooking food which would normally be grilled under a radiant grill. It uses the fan element ONLY (not the radiant grill element) on a fairly high setting with the door closed. The hot air circulating around the food seals it quickly and gives an even crispness on both sides without the need for turning. Usually the food is placed on a grid shelf with a tray underneath to catch the drips.

Hot air grilling can be used for small pieces of meat (e.g. chops, kebabs, sausages, chicken portions, mixed grill), fish and toasted sandwiches. In fact almost everything, some exceptions being toast, gratin dishes, brûlées and rare steak.

This method of cooking is ideal for party food and barbecues. By placing a drip tray on the bottom runner more than one rack of food can be cooked at the same time. Even if cooking only one tray of food it does mean that the rest of the meal can be cooked at the same time, thus making it very economical and time saving.

Vegetable accompaniments such as mushrooms and tomatoes may be cooked in the drip tray underneath the grid. Because cooking times and temperatures are less critical, foods do not burn or spoil so quickly. The cooking process is more gentle with less splattering of fat and juices, although if the drip tray is not being used it is quite safe to line it with foil to aid cleaning or, if your oven allows it, to put water in the tray as for roasting.

For flat fish and toasties, a solid baking tray lined with baking parchment can be used. The heat circulating underneath the tray will cook the underside.

Timings and temperatures

A temperature of 190°C or over should usually be used, depending on the degree of crispness required. If your oven has the range, a very high temperature (200–250°C) will give a darker, crisper, barbecue-type finish but the food should be watched carefully as cooking times will be slightly less. However, a lower temperature of 180°C is recommended when cooking more delicate items such as fish fillets or when using the rest of the oven for general cooking and desserts.

Most hot air grilling can be done from a cold oven unless cooking steak, in which case the tray can also be heated. Personally I prefer to preheat for 5–8 minutes for red meats and toasties. Rare steaks are best cooked conventionally under a radiant grill.

Because there is no radiant heat the food will need a little longer to cook, approximately 15–25 additional minutes, depending on the number of trays being cooked. However, the main advantage is that food does not have to be turned or basted and more food can be cooked at the same time.

A Guide to Cooking Using Hot Air Grilling

Food	Time	Temperature
Bacon	15–20 minutes	190–200°C
Beefburgers	25–30 minutes	190–200°C
Chicken portions	35–45 minutes	190–200°C
Cod steaks	15–20 minutes	180–290°C
Fish fingers	20–25 minutes	200°C
Filleted fish	12–15 minutes	180°C
Kebabs	30–35 minutes	190°C
Kidneys	35–40 minutes	180°C
Lamb chops	25–35 minutes	190–200°C
Liver	35–40 minutes	180°C
Oven chips	15–20 minutes	200–210°C
Pork chops	35–40 minutes	190–200°C
Sausages (large)	25–30 minutes	200°C
Small whole fish	15–20 minutes	180–190°C
Steaks (medium to well done)	15–20 minutes	200°C
Toasted sandwiches	15–20 minutes	190–220°C

Season meat with herbs and pepper and brush with a little oil if very lean. Brush fish with a little melted butter and a sprinkle of lemon juice.

Remember that a selection of dishes in this section may be cooked together either on separate levels or sharing the same one.

Chicken Kebabs

SERVES 4

✳

4 boneless chicken breasts, skinned
12 streaky bacon rashers (slices)
100 g/4 oz/2 cups button mushrooms (optional)

For the marinade:
30 ml/2 tbsp olive oil
30 ml/2 tbsp tomato ketchup (catsup)
30 ml/2 tbsp soy sauce
Good pinch of garlic salt
Good pinch of ground ginger
15 ml/1 tbsp brown sugar
Pinch of mustard powder
Freshly ground black pepper

1 Mix the marinade ingredients in a basin.

2 Cut the chicken into 2.5 cm (1 in) cubes and stir into the marinade. Leave for 1 hour in the fridge.

3 Wash the mushrooms, remove and discard stalks, and cut in half.

④ Stretch the bacon rashers out with the back of a knife. Cut in half and roll each piece up.

⑤ Thread alternate pieces of bacon, chicken and mushroom on to small metal skewers. Brush all over with remaining marinade and place on a metal grid above a drip tray. Hot air grill.

TEMP	TIME
190–210°C (preheat for 8 minutes)	20–25 minutes

COOK'S NOTE
Vary these kebabs by adding small sausages or pieces of hamburger – children will love them.

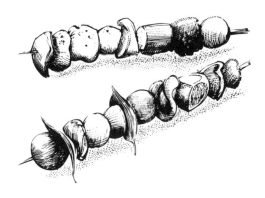

CRUNCHY CHICKEN

COURTESY OF AEG LTD

SERVES 4

8 chicken drumsticks OR thighs
1 egg, beaten
60 ml/4 tbsp breadcrumbs
5 ml/1 tsp chopped fresh parsley
75 g/3 oz/²/₃ cup Cheddar cheese, grated
2.5 ml/¹/₂ tsp garlic salt
5 ml/1 tsp paprika
Salt and freshly ground black pepper

1 Dip the chicken pieces in beaten egg.

2 Mix together all the other ingredients and use to coat the chicken thoroughly.

3 Place the portions on a metal grid above a drip tray and hot air grill.

TEMP	TIME
190–220°C	40–45 minutes (from cold) OR 35–40 minutes (if preheated)

SESAME DRUMSTICKS

COURTESY OF NEFF (UK) LTD

SERVES 4

✳

12 chicken drumsticks OR thighs

For the glaze:
25 g/1 oz/2 tbsp sesame seeds
Juice of 1 lemon
75 g/3 oz/$^1/_3$ cup butter
30 ml/2 tbsp clear honey
Pinch of chilli powder

1 Heat the glaze ingredients in a microwave on a low setting or gently in a saucepan until the butter has melted.

2 Glaze the chicken drumsticks thoroughly, sprinkle with sesame seeds and place on a grid above a drip tray.

3 Hot air grill.

TEMP	TIME
180°C	40 minutes (if preheated) OR 45 minutes (from cold)

TANDOORI-STYLE CHICKEN

SERVES 4

❋

4 chicken joints
10 ml/2 tsp lemon juice
2.5 ml/¹/₂ tsp salt

For the marinade:
2 garlic cloves, crushed
30 ml/2 tbsp tandoori spice
150 g/5 fl oz/²/₃ cup natural (plain) yoghurt
30 ml/2 tbsp wine vinegar
30 ml/2 tbsp olive oil
Juice of 1 lemon
30 ml/2 tbsp tomato purée (paste)

1 Remove the skin from the chicken joints and using a sharp knife make several deep slashes across the flesh. Rub in the salt and lemon juice.

2 Put the chicken into a dish with the garlic. Mix all the other ingredients together and pour over the chicken. Leave to marinate for at least 3 hours, preferably overnight.

3 Hot air grill.

TEMP	TIME
190°C (preheat for 5–8 minutes)	30–45 minutes, depending on the size of joints (drumsticks and thighs will need only 30 minutes; leg or breast joints 45 minutes)

CHICKEN OR BEEF SATAY

COURTESY OF NEFF (UK) LTD

SERVES 6

750 g/1¹/₂ lb boneless chicken breasts OR rump steak
10 ml/2 tsp coriander (cilantro)
5 ml/1 tsp ground cumin
5 ml/1 tsp ground turmeric
5 ml/1 tsp chilli powder
5 ml/1 tsp grated lemon rind
5 ml/1 tsp sugar
100 g/4 oz/¹/₂ cup peanut butter
15 ml/1 tbsp oil
30 ml/2 tbsp grated coconut

1 Trim the meat and cut into 2.5 cm (1in) cubes.

2 Mix together all the spices and the lemon rind and sugar. Toss the meat in the mixture until thoroughly coated and leave for at least 1 hour.

3 Thread the cubes on to 6 skewers.

4 Combine the peanut butter, oil and grated coconut. Coat the meat with the sauce and marinate for at least 2 hours.

5 Place the skewers on a wire grid above a drip tray. Hot air grill until tender.

TEMP	TIME
190°C	20 minutes (if preheated) OR 25 minutes (from cold)

VEGETABLE KEBABS

SERVES 6

✳

1 yellow (bell) pepper, seeded and cut into pieces
1 red (bell) pepper, seeded and cut into pieces
3 courgettes (zucchini)
100 g/4 oz/2 cups button mushrooms
12 cherry tomatoes
Olive oil, for brushing
5 ml/1 tsp oregano OR chopped fresh parsley

1 Blanch the pepper pieces in boiling water or in a microwave for 2 minutes. Chop the courgettes (zucchini) into thick slices, approx. 2.5 cm (1 in). Trim the stalks off the mushrooms and discard.

2 Thread alternate pieces of each vegetable on to ten or twelve small skewers.

3 Brush all surfaces liberally with the oil. Sprinkle with the herbs.

4 Place on a grid above a drip tray and hot air grill.

TEMP	TIME
190°C	20 minutes (if preheated) OR 25 minutes (from cold)

CHEESEY COD STEAKS

SERVES 4

4 cod OR haddock steaks

25 g/1 oz/2 tbsp butter, melted

Juice of $^1/_2$ lemon

100 g/4 oz/1 cup grated cheese

Salt and freshly ground pepper

Chopped fresh parsley

1 tomato, sliced

1 Place fish steaks on a lined baking sheet brushed with the melted butter. Sprinkle with the lemon juice and top with grated cheese. Season and sprinkle with the parsley.

2 Place two slices of tomato on each steak.

3 Open hot air grill.

TEMP	TIME
180°C	15–20 minutes (if preheated) OR 20–25 minutes (from cold)

BARBECUE-STYLE SPARE RIBS

SERVES 4

✳

12–16 pork spare ribs

For the marinade:

30 ml/2 tbsp clear honey

45 ml/3 tbsp soy sauce

45 ml/3 tbsp wine vinegar

30 ml/2 tbsp tomato purée (paste)

Salt

300 ml/^{1}/$_2$ pt/1^1/$_4$ cups stock

Chopped fresh parsley

① Place the ribs in an ovenproof dish.

② Mix together all the marinade ingredients. Pour over the ribs and leave overnight, turning occasionally if possible.

③ Cover the dish with foil and cook the ribs and marinade in the oven.

TEMP	TIME
165°C (no need to preheat)	1^1/$_2$ hours

④ Remove the dish from the oven. Lift out the ribs and put on a metal grid with a drip tray underneath. Hot air grill.

⑤ Meanwhile, sieve the juices into a large pan and boil to reduce the liquid until thickened and serve as a sauce.

6 Remove the ribs and place on a warm serving dish. Pour a little of the sauce over and sprinkle with the parsley.

TEMP	TIME
190–200°C (already hot)	20 minutes

PORK CHOPS

SERVES 4

✳

4 pork chops OR steaks
Chopped fresh parsley
Pinch of garlic salt
Pinch of chopped fresh tarragon
25 g/1 oz/2 tbsp butter

1 Trim excess fat off the chops and place them on a grid above a drip tray.

2 Sprinkle with the herbs, garlic salt and seasoning. Top with a knob of butter.

3 Hot air grill.

TEMP	TIME
190°C	35–40 minutes (if preheated) OR 40–45 minutes (from cold)

STUFFED PORK CHOPS

As above, but make a slit in the side of the chop and stuff with a little parsley and thyme stuffing made up from approxi-mately half a packet.

STUFFED PORK FILLETS

SERVES 4

✳

1 small cooking (tart) apple

150 g/5 oz/²/₃ cup cranberry sauce

2 pork tenderloins

Salt and freshly ground black pepper

25 g/1 oz/2 tbsp butter

30 ml/2 tbsp clear honey

1 Peel and chop the apple and mix with the cranberry sauce.

2 Trim the fillets and cut away the silver threads.

3 Cut the fillets lengthways without cutting through and gently open out. Spread the cranberry and apple along one of the fillets, season and place the other on top.

4 Tie the fillets together with string at each end and in the middle.

5 Melt the butter and honey together gently and spread over the fillets.

6 Hot air grill.

TEMP	TIME
190–210°C (for best results preheat for 5–8 minutes)	30–40 minutes

SWEET GAMMON STEAKS

SERVES 4

✳

4 gammon steaks

50 g/2 oz/¹/₄ cup butter

25 g/1 oz/2 tbsp brown sugar

2.5 ml/¹/₂ tsp made mustard

1 Melt the butter and sugar together. Stir in the mustard.

2 Brush one side of each gammon steak and lay brushed-side down on a grid or baking sheet. The grid can be lined with foil if you wish.

3 Brush the top side with the remaining butter mixture. Hot air grill.

TEMP	TIME
190–200°C	20–25 minutes (if preheated) OR 25–30 minutes (from cold)

FAN-TAIL SAUSAGES

❋

Chipolata sausages
Barbecue OR tomato sauce, for dipping

1 Using scissors cut the sausages lengthways from each end, leaving about 2.5 cm (1 in) still joined in the centre.

2 Place on a grid above a drip tray and hot air grill.

TEMP	TIME
190°C	20–25 minutes (if preheated) OR 25–30 minutes (from cold)

MINTED LAMB CHOPS

SERVES 4

❋

4 lamb chops OR cutlets

25 g/1 oz/2 tbsp butter

5 ml/1 tsp dried OR chopped fresh mint

1 Wipe and trim the lamb chops and make a small slit on the top of each one.

2 Soften the butter and mix with the mint. Using a knife push some butter into each slit allowing some to overflow on top of the meat.

3 Place cutlets on a grid above a drip tray and hot air grill.

TEMP	TIME
190°C	25 minutes (if preheated) OR 30 minutes (from cold)

Lamb Cutlets in Herb Breadcrumbs

SERVES 8

✳

8 lamb cutlets

175 g/6 oz/3 cups fresh wholemeal breadcrumbs

5 ml/1 tsp chopped fresh parsley

5 ml/1 tsp dried mixed herbs

3 eggs

Salt and freshly ground black pepper

1 Mix the breadcrumbs, parsley, mixed herbs, salt and pepper in a bowl.

2 Beat the eggs together in a shallow dish.

3 Trim the excess fat from the cutlets. Dip each in the egg to coat well.

4 Cover with the breadcrumbs, herbs and seasoning.

5 Lay the cutlets on an oven grid and position over the drip tray.

5 Hot air grill.

TEMP	TIME
190–200°C	25–30 minutes (if preheated) OR 30–35 minutes (from cold)

LAMB KEBABS

SERVES 4

✳

1 kg/2 lb approx. fillet end of a leg of lamb
1 yellow (bell) pepper
1 red (bell) pepper
1 large onion
4 lambs' kidneys
6 plum tomatoes, halved
12 button mushrooms

For the marinade:
275 ml/^{1}/$_2$ pt/1^1/$_4$ cups passata (sieved tomatoes)
30 ml/2 tbsp clear honey
45 ml/3 tbsp wine vinegar
1 garlic clove, crushed
45 ml/3 tbsp soy sauce
275 ml/^{1}/$_2$ pt/1^1/$_4$ cups chicken stock
Salt and freshly ground black pepper
10 ml/2 tsp dried mixed herbs
15 ml/1 tbsp olive oil

1 Bone the lamb, trim off the skin and excess fat and cut into approximately 3.5 cm (1^1/$_2$ in) cubes. Halve the kidneys and trim off any fat.

2 Combine all the marinade ingredients together in a bowl and add the meat. Cover with clingfilm (plastic wrap) and leave for at least 3 hours or overnight if possible.

3 Peel the onion and cut into wedges. Remove the seeds from the peppers and cut into 3.5 cm (1^1/$_2$ in) pieces. Blanch the peppers and onions in boiling water for 2–3 minutes, drain and cool, or blanch in a microwave for 1 minute on full power.

4 Thread the lamb, kidney halves and vegetables on to skewers.

5 Place on a grid above a drip tray. Brush well with some of the marinade.

6 Hot air grill.

7 Meanwhile, pour the remaining marinade through a sieve into a large saucepan, bring to the boil and simmer until liquid reduces to a sauce consistency. Serve the kebabs on a bed of rice with a green salad. Serve the sauce separately.

TEMP	TIME
190°C (preheat for 5–8 minutes)	30 minutes

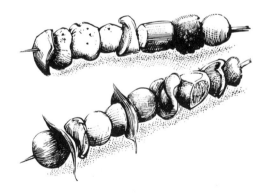

TOAST HAWAII

COURTESY OF BOSCH (UK) LTD

SERVES 4 AS A SNACK

❋

4 thick slices of bread

4 slices cooked ham

4 pineapple rings, drained

50 g/2 oz/¹/₂ cup Cheddar cheese, grated

Freshly ground black pepper

1 Butter the bread on both sides.

2 Cover each slice with a piece of ham, then a pineapple ring and top with the cheese.

3 Season with pepper and hot air grill.

TEMP	TIME
190°C (preheat for 5–8 minutes)	15–20 minutes

TUNA FISH TOASTIES

COURTESY OF NEFF (UK) LTD

SERVES 6

✳

6 thick slices of bread

50 g/2 oz/$^1/_4$ cup soft margarine

175 g/6 oz/1 small can tuna

50 g/2 oz/4 tbsp mayonnaise

75 g/3 oz/$^2/_3$ cup Cheddar cheese, grated

Salt and freshly ground black pepper

1 Spread one side of each slice with margarine. Place buttered-side down on a wire rack or baking sheet lined with greaseproof (waxed) paper.

2 Drain the tuna well and mix with the mayonnaise. Season.

3 Spread the tuna mix over the bread.

4 Sprinkle with the cheese.

5 Hot air grill.

TEMP	TIME
190°C (preheat for 5–8 minutes)	20 minutes
COOK'S NOTE	
Vary these toasties by substituting the same quantity of tinned red salmon for the tuna.	

COX'S CHEESE AND NUT TOASTIES

COURTESY OF NEFF (UK) LTD

SERVES 4

2 Cox's eating (dessert) apples
225 g/8 oz/2 cups Cheddar cheese, grated
Dash of Worcestershire sauce
4 thick slices of bread
50 g/2 oz/2 tbsp soft margarine
25 g/1 oz/$^1/_4$ cup walnuts, chopped

1 Peel and grate the apples into a bowl.

2 Mix the cheese and grated apple with a few drops of Worcestershire sauce.

3 Spread one side of the bread with margarine. Place on grease-proof (waxed) paper on a rack or baking sheet, buttered side down.

4 Spread the unbuttered side of the bread with the cheese mixture and sprinkle with chopped nuts.

5 Place the sandwiches on a wire rack above a drip tray and cook until the cheese has melted. Cut into triangles and serve.

TEMP	TIME
180–190°C (preheat for 5–8 minutes)	15–20 minutes

BAKING

Follow the guidelines in the temperature charts and remember that the fat filter, if your oven has one, should be removed for baking.

The oven does not usually need to be preheated. However, preheating for 5–8 minutes gives a better result for certain items:

- Light cakes with a short cooking time (e.g. Swiss (jelly) rolls, *petits fours*, biscuits)
- Yeast mixtures or scones, which need a hot oven to prevent the yeast from over-rising or to bring the scones up quickly to keep their centres soft
- Soufflés
- Batch baking of more than two trays

Be aware that:
- If you are used to a gas or conventional electric oven you may be surprised by the reduced degree of browning on cakes. Do not be tempted to raise the temperature or, though they may appear cooked on the outside, they will not be cooked in the centre and will sink on removal from the oven
- If during baking (especially from a cold oven) dishes seem to be browning unevenly there is no need to panic. If your temperature is correct browning will even out by the time the food is cooked. Uneven cooking which does *not* correct itself is more likely to be due to setting too high a temperature rather than a faulty oven

Batch Baking
Batch baking saves not only time but also fuel, and a variety of items can be baked then frozen and used as required. Either make up a large quantity of one mixture and make a selection of similar items or choose a variety of different items that may be cooked at the same time.

Guidelines for successful batch baking

1 Preheat for 8 minutes when planning to bake more than two trays at a time. Generally all four shelves can be used but the most even colouring is obtained by using only three shelves.

2 Foods that require different times and or temperatures may still be cooked together. Providing the difference is not greater than 15°C, bake at the average temperature required for all the different dishes or the temperature of the most delicate item.

3 Don't forget, it is possible to remove food from the oven without the remaining items spoiling.

4 When the oven is fully loaded a slight increase in time (10–15 minutes) may be necessary because the movement of air will be slowed a little by the trays and tins.

5 Stagger the positions of the food as much as possible and make sure that your own trays do not overlap the oven racks at the sides or front as this may impede the air flow.

6 Be aware that different baking tins and sheets do affect results.

7 One batch of cakes can be put into the oven while others are being prepared. Be aware that the first cakes will take a few minutes longer than subsequent batches because the oven will not be quite up to temperature.

8 Pies and flans with a pastry (paste) base are best cooked in metal flan tins rather than ovenproof glass or earthenware, which are poor conductors of heat.

9 If your oven comes with solid baking sheets and wire racks, alternate these to allow maximum movement of air.

FRUIT SCONES

MAKES 10–12

※

450 g/1 lb/4 cups self-raising (self-rising) flour
5 ml/1 tsp baking powder
100 g/4 oz/¹/₂ cup block margarine
50 g/2 oz/¹/₄ cup lard
100 g/4 oz/¹/₂ cup caster (superfine) sugar
175 g/6 oz/1 cup mixed dried fruit (fruit cake mix)
300 ml/¹/₂ pt/1¹/₄ cups milk

1 Sieve together the flour and baking powder. Rub in the fats until the mixture resembles fine breadcrumbs.

2 Add the sugar and fruit and mix with the milk to form a soft dough.

3 Knead gently on a floured board and roll out to 2 cm (³/₄ in) thick. Use a 6 cm (2¹/₂ in) cutter to make 10–12 scones. Brush with a little milk.

4 Bake.

TEMP	TIME
190–200°C (preheat for 5–8 minutes)	15–20 minutes

COOK'S NOTES
Once cooked, scones freeze well. Why not double the quantity and vary the flavourings? Omit fruit and add cherries OR chopped walnuts and dates OR 100 g/4 oz/1 cup grated Cheddar cheese.

VICTORIA SANDWICH CAKE

SERVES 8–10

✳

175 g/6 oz/³/₄ cup caster (superfine) sugar
175 g/6 oz/³/₄ cup block margarine OR butter, softened
3 eggs
175 g/6 oz/1¹/₂ cups self-raising (self-rising) flour
Warm water
Jam (conserve), for spreading
Icing (confectioners') sugar, for sprinkling

1 Prepare 2 × 18–20 cm (7–8 in) sandwich tins by greasing with a little margarine and lining with a circle of greaseproof (waxed) paper.

2 Cream the sugar and butter together until light and fluffy (this takes time but is worth the effort).

3 Gradually beat in the eggs a little at a time. If the mixture begins to curdle add 15 ml/1 tbsp sieved flour.

4 Gradually fold in the remaining flour with a metal spoon. The mixture should have a dropping consistency; if too stiff add a little of the water. It should NOT pour.

5 Spoon equally into the tins and spread gently with a palette knife. Bake.

6 When cool, sandwich together with jam and sprinkle sieved icing sugar on top .

NB: Flavourings can be varied by adding the juice and grated rind of one orange, or a few drops of vanilla essence, or replace 25 g/1 oz/ 2 tbsp of the flour with 25 g/1 oz/2 tbsp of cocoa (unsweetened chocolate) powder.

TEMP	TIME
160–170°C	25–30 minutes (if preheated) OR 30–35 minutes (from cold)

COOK'S NOTES
The mixture can be made using the all-in-one method, using soft margarine in the recipe and mixing all the ingredients together until smooth (about 2 minutes). If using a food processor, add ½ level tsp of baking powder for every 100 g/4 oz/1 cup flour. These mixtures all freeze well, so double or treble the quantities for a batch bake.

FAIRY CAKES

MAKES 12–15

✳

**1 × 100 g/4 oz/1 cup quantity Victoria sandwich mix
(see page 78)**

1 Put a large heaped teaspoonful of the mixture into each of the paper cake cases (cupcake papers) or bun tin (muffin pan) sections.

2 Bake until well risen and firm to the touch.

TEMP	TIME
170°C	15–20 minutes (if preheated) OR 20–25 minutes (from cold)

APPLE CAKE

SERVES 10–15

✳

1 × 175 g/6 oz/1¼ cup quantity Victoria sandwich mix
(see page 78)

15 ml/1 tbsp caster (superfine) sugar

5 ml/1 tsp ground cinnamon

3 eating (dessert) apples (Golden Delicious
or Cox's Orange Pippin)

❶ Grease a baking tin approximately 18 × 28 cm (7 × 11 in) and 5–7.5 cm (2–3 in) deep and sprinkle a light coating of flour on the sides and base.

❷ Spoon the mixture into the tin and spread evenly with a palette knife.

❸ Mix together the sugar and cinnamon.

❹ Peel and core the apples. Cut into quarters and slice thinly.

❺ Arrange the slices of apple in rows across the cake mixture. Sprinkle with the sugar and cinnamon and bake. Allow to cool a little in the tin then cut into squares and serve warm or cold.

TEMP	TIME
160–170°C	30–40 minutes (if preheated) OR 40–45 minutes (from cold)

SWISS ROLL

SERVES 8–10

✳

3 eggs, at room temperature
75 g/3 oz/$^1/_3$ cup caster (superfine) sugar
75 g/3 oz/$^2/_3$ cup self-raising (self-rising) flour
30–45 ml/2–3 tbsp raspberry jam (conserve)
Caster (superfine) sugar, for sprinkling

1. Grease and line a Swiss (jelly) roll tin. Also grease the lining paper.

2. Whisk the eggs and sugar together over hot water (to speed up the process) until the mixture is thick and creamy, and leaves a trail when the whisk is removed.

3. Sieve the flour and fold gently into the mixture a little at a time using a 'figure of eight' movement.

4. Pour the mixture into the tin, tipping it from side to side to spread evenly (do not use a knife).

5. Bake.

6. Meanwhile prepare a suitable surface by laying out a damp tea towel (dish cloth) covered with a sheet of greaseproof (waxed) paper sprinkled with caster sugar. Warm some raspberry jam for spreading.

7. When cooked (light brown and springy to touch) turn out on to the sugared paper, remove lining and trim the edges with a sharp knife if necessary. Spread with the warm jam.

⑧ Working quickly, make a slit across the bottom short end of the sponge 1 cm ($^1/_2$ in) from the edge. DO NOT cut all the way through. Fold this edge in first, then roll, first with the fingers then continue by drawing the paper away from you over the sponge. Leave to cool, resting on the seam. Dredge with caster sugar.

TEMP	TIME
190°C (preheat for 8 minutes)	8–10 minutes

CHOCOLATE SWISS ROLL

Substitute 25 g/1 oz/2 tbsp of the flour with the same amount of sieved cocoa (unsweetened chocolate) powder. When baked, roll up with a sheet of greaseproof paper inside. Unroll gently when cool then fill with butter cream.

FRUIT FLAN

SERVES 8–10

❋

**1 × 75 g/3 oz/²/₃ cup quantity Victoria sandwich sponge mix
(see page 78)**

1 × 400 g/14 oz can peach slices in juice

1 packet quick-setting jel mix

1 Grease a flan tin (pie shell) (with a raised centre) thoroughly and dust with flour.

2 Pour in the mixture and bake. Turn out upside-down on to a cooling rack. Allow to cool.

3 Drain and reserve the juice from the peaches and arrange attractively in the centre of the flan. Make up the jel mix from the packet instructions, using fruit juice instead of water.

4 Pour over the peaches. If preferred, half a packet of orange jelly can be used with the juice instead.

5 Decorate with swirls of piped whipped cream.

TEMP	TIME
170°C (preheat for 8 minutes)	25–30 minutes

COOK'S NOTE
Make an extra flan and freeze for use at a later date as a Baked Alaska (see page 174) or as a base for a trifle.

MADELEINES

MAKES 8–10

**1 × 75 g/3 oz/²/₃ cup quantity Victoria sandwich mix
(see page 78)**

50 g/2 oz/¹/₂ cup desiccated (shredded) coconut

Raspberry OR apricot jam (conserve)

Glacé (candied) cherries, for decoration

1 Grease dariole moulds or deep bun tins. Half-fill with mixture.

2 Bake.

3 When cool, coat with jam and roll in the coconut.

4 Decorate with half a cherry.

TEMP	TIME
190°C (preheat for 6–8 minutes)	10–15 minutes
COOK'S NOTE	
As some children do not like coconut or cherries, try rolling the Madeleines in hundreds and thousands and putting a small sweet on top.	

CHOUX PASTRY

USE FOR CHOCOLATE ECLAIRS, PROFITEROLES, PARIS BREST, CREAM PUFFS

✳

50 g/2 oz/^{1}/$_4$ cup butter
150 ml/^{1}/$_4$ pt/^{2}/$_3$ cup water
5 ml/1 tsp caster (superfine) sugar
100 g/4 oz/1 cup plain (all-purpose) flour
3 eggs, whisked together

1 Place the butter, water and sugar in a saucepan, melt over a gentle heat then bring to the boil.

2 Remove from the heat, add the flour and stir in well.

3 Return to the heat, beat well until the mixture forms a ball in the middle of the pan and leaves the side of the pan clear.

4 Put the hot dough in a basin and beat in the eggs with a wooden spoon until the mixture is soft but stiff enough to hold its shape when dropped off the spoon.

5 Beat until the dough shines.

CHOCOLATE ECLAIRS

1 Fill a piping bag fitted with a 1 cm (^{1}/$_2$ in) plain nozzle with the dough and pipe in 7.5 cm (3 in) lengths on to baking sheets lined with non-stick baking parchment or greased and sprinkled with water. Leave a space between each. Bake.

2 Make a slit along one side of each éclair to allow the steam to escape. Leave to cool.

③ When cool, fill with sweetened whipped cream and coat with Chocolate Icing (page 87) or melted chocolate.

TEMP	TIME
180–190°C (preheat for 5–8 minutes)	20–25 minutes

PROFITEROLES

Prepare as for Chocolate Eclairs, but pipe small balls about the size of a walnut.

CHOCOLATE ICING

50 g/2 oz plain (semi-sweet) chocolate
10 g/^{1}/$_2$ oz/^{1}/$_2$ tbsp butter
30 ml/2 tbsp warm water
175 g/6 oz/1 cup icing (confectioners') sugar, sifted

① Gently heat the chocolate with the butter in a basin over a pan of hot water until melted OR melt on the low setting of a microwave.

② Remove from the heat and beat in the icing sugar and warm water. When smooth, dip the top of the éclairs into the icing to coat them.

PARIS BREST

*

1 quantity choux pastry (paste) (see page 86)
1 egg, beaten
Flaked almonds, for sprinkling
300 ml/^{1}/$_2$ pt/1^1/$_4$ cups double (heavy) cream
10 ml/2 tsp caster (superfine) sugar
Vanilla essence
Fresh soft fruit, for filling
Icing (confectioners') sugar, for dredging

1 Spoon the pastry into a 20–23 cm (8–9 in) ring or pipe a double circle with the same size nozzle as for profiteroles.

2 Brush with a little egg and sprinkle with a few flaked almonds.

3 Bake.

4 Split the cake horizontally. Scoop out any uncooked centre and return the halves to the oven for 5 minutes.

5 When cool, fill with sweetened whipped cream flavoured with vanilla essence and fruit. Sandwich together. Sprinkle icing sugar over the top.

TEMP	TIME
190–200°C (preheat for 8 minutes)	45 minutes

CREAM PUFFS

⁕

1 quantity choux pastry (paste) (see page 86)
150 ml/¹/₄ pt/²/₃ cup double (heavy) cream
Icing (confectioners') sugar, for sprinkling

1 Pipe rounds of pastry about 5 cm (2 in) in diameter on to a lined or greased oven tray about 7.5 cm (3 in) apart. Cover with a deep cake tin and bake.

2 When cold, make a slit in the side of each one and fill with whipped cream, then either sprinkle with icing sugar or ice with water icing.

TEMP	TIME
190–200°C (preheat for 8 minutes)	35 minutes

DATE AND WALNUT CAKE

COURTESY OF GAGGENAU UK LTD

SERVES 10–12

❋

150 ml/^{1}/$_4$ pt/^{2}/$_3$ cup hot water
225 g/8 oz/1^1/$_3$ cups dried stoned dates, halved
100 g/4 oz/^{1}/$_2$ cup butter
100 g/4 oz/^{1}/$_2$ cup caster (superfine) sugar
30 ml/2 tbsp golden (light corn) syrup
2 large eggs
275 g/10 oz/2^1/$_2$ cups self-raising (self-rising) flour
2.5 ml/^{1}/$_2$ tsp mixed (apple-pie) spice
50 g/2 oz/^{1}/$_2$ cup walnuts, chopped
Walnuts, chopped, for decoration

1 Grease and line a deep 20 cm (8 in) round cake tin or 18 cm (7 in) square tin.

2 Pour the hot water on to three quarters of the dates and set aside.

3 Cream the butter and sugar together until light and fluffy. Add the syrup then the eggs, one at a time, beating well between each addition. Sieve the flour and spice and gently fold into the mixture.

4 Add the dates with the water and the halved walnuts. Mix until the dates and nuts are evenly distributed and put the mixture into the tin. Spread evenly and decorate with remaining dates and chopped walnuts.

5 Bake.

TEMP	TIME
160–170°C (no need to preheat)	1^1/$_4$ hours

CHERRY AND COCONUT CAKE

MAKES 2 LOAVES

※

350 g/12 oz/1¹/₂ cups glacé (candied) cherries
50 g/2 oz/¹/₂ cup desiccated (shredded) coconut
200 g/7 oz/³/₄ cup butter
350 g/12 oz/3 cups self-raising (self-rising) flour
200 g/7 oz/³/₄ cup caster (superfine) sugar
Salt
2 large eggs
150 ml/¹/₄ pt/²/₃ cup milk
Sugar, for sprinkling
Desiccated (shredded) coconut, for sprinkling

1 Prepare 2 × 450 g/1 lb loaf tins by greasing with butter, placing a piece of greaseproof (waxed) paper cut to size in the base and coating with a sprinkling of flour.

2 Wash the cherries to remove the syrup, dry thoroughly on kitchen paper, cut in half and roll in the coconut.

3 Rub the butter into the flour until the mixture resembles fine breadcrumbs and then add the sugar, salt, cherries and coconut and mix together.

4 Beat the eggs with the milk and add to the dry ingredients. Mix gently together.

5 Divide the mixture evenly between the tins, sprinkle a little coconut and sugar on to the surface and bake until golden and firm to the touch.

TEMP	TIME
160–170°C (no need to preheat)	45 minutes

SACHERTORTE
(A rich chocolate cake)

COURTESY OF AEG (UK) LTD

SERVES 10–12

✳

150 g/5 oz plain (semi-sweet) chocolate
3 egg whites
150 g/5 oz/²/₃ cup butter
150 g/5 oz/1¹/₄ cups caster (superfine) sugar
6 egg yolks
120 g/4¹/₂ oz/1 large cup self-raising (self-rising) flour

For the filling:
50 g/2 oz/2 tbsp apricot jam (conserve)

For the topping:
50 g/2 oz/1¹/₂ cups melted chocolate OR chocolate cake covering

1 Grease and line two 18 cm (7 in) cake tins.

2 Break the chocolate into small pieces and melt in a bowl over hot water or on the low setting of a microwave.

3 Beat the egg whites in a separate bowl until stiff.

4 Cream the fat, sugar and egg yolks in another bowl until light and fluffy. Fold in the melted chocolate and half the sifted flour. Fold in the remaining flour together with the beaten egg whites.

5 Pour the mixture into the tins and bake until firm to the touch.

6 When cool, sandwich together with apricot jam and cover the top with the melted cake covering.

TEMP	TIME
160–170°C (preheat for 5–8 minutes)	25–30 minutes
COOK'S NOTE	
This torte tastes better if left for 2–3 days before cutting.	

MERINGUES

MAKES 10

✳

2 egg whites
100 g/4 oz/¹/₂ cup caster (superfine) sugar
150 ml/¹/₄ pt/²/₃ cup double (heavy) cream

1 Whisk the egg whites until stiff. Add half the sugar and whisk well. Lightly fold in the remaining sugar.

2 Either pipe or spoon 20 small rounds on to a baking sheet lined with non-stick baking parchment.

3 Bake until dried out.

4 When cold, sandwich together with the whipped cream.

TEMP	TIME
80–90°C (no need to preheat)	2¹/₂–3 hours

MINCE PIES

MAKES 10–12

❋

For the pastry (paste):
225 g/8 oz/2 cups plain (all-purpose) flour
100 g/4 oz/^{1}/$_2$ cup margarine
Salt
10 ml/2 tsp caster (superfine) sugar
30 ml/2 tbsp cold water

For the filling:
350 g/12 oz/1 cup mincemeat
15 ml/1 tbsp brandy

1 Rub the margarine into the flour and salt until the mixture resembles fine breadcrumbs. Add the sugar, then, using a round-blade knife, mix in enough water to form a soft dough. Knead lightly, cover with cling film (plastic wrap) and allow to rest in a refrigerator for 30 minutes.

2 Mix the mincemeat with the brandy.

3 Using slightly more than half the pastry, roll out and cut 10–12 rounds using a 6 cm (2^1/$_2$ in) fluted cutter. Line the tartlet (patty) tins.

4 Fill each with a heaped teaspoonful of mincemeat.

5 Roll out the remaining pastry and cut out the lids with either a 5 cm (2 in) fluted or fancy shape cutter. Place lids on and brush with a little milk.

6 Bake.

TEMP	TIME
180°C (preheat for 8 minutes)	20 minutes

COOK'S NOTES

I find smaller, loose lids allow the steam to escape and the mincemeat is less likely to bubble over. A slit in the top is not always sufficient especially if, like me, you like plenty of mincemeat in your pies!
A lattice cutter can also be used.

CHRISTMAS OR SPECIAL OCCASION CAKE

❄

	For a 20 cm (8 in) square OR 23 cm (9 in) round cake	For a 25 cm (10 in) square OR 28cm (11 in) round cake
Currants	375 g/13 oz/2^1/$_4$ cups	550 g/1^1/$_4$ lb/3^1/$_3$ cups
Sultanas (golden raisins)	250 g/9 oz/1^1/$_2$ cups	370 g/13oz/2^1/$_4$ cups
Raisins	150 g/5 oz/1 cup	200 g/7 oz/1^1/$_4$ cups
Sherry, brandy OR orange juice	45 ml/3 tbsp	60 ml/4 tbsp
Glacé (candied) cherries, washed, dried and chopped	75 g/3 oz/^{1}/$_3$ cup	100 g/4 oz/^{1}/$_2$ cup
Mixed peel, chopped	40 g/1^1/$_2$ oz/^{1}/$_4$ cup	50 g/2 oz/^{1}/$_3$ cup
Blanched almonds, chopped	40 g/1^1/$_2$ oz/^{1}/$_4$ cup	50 g/2 oz/^{1}/$_3$ cup
Ground almonds	75 g/3 oz/^{3}/$_4$ cup	100 g/4 oz/1 cup
Lemon, grated rind only	1	1
Orange, grated rind only	1	1
Plain (all-purpose) flour	250 g/9 oz/2^1/$_4$ cups	450 g/14 oz/3^1/$_2$ cups
Mixed (apple-pie) spice	10 ml/2 tsp	10 ml/2 tsp
Grated nutmeg	5 ml/1 tsp	5 ml/1 tsp
Salt	2.5 ml/^{1}/$_2$ tsp	2.5 ml/^{1}/$_2$ tsp

Butter OR **block** margarine	225 g/8 oz/1 cup	350 g/12 oz/1¹/₂ cups
Soft brown sugar	225 g/8 oz/1 cup	350 g/12 oz/1¹/₂ cups
Eggs	5	7
Black treacle (molasses)	15 ml/1tbsp	30 ml/2 tbsp

1 Grease the tin and line with a double layer of greaseproof (waxed) paper extending about 5 cm(2 in) above the tin. Grease well, then tie a double layer of newspaper around the tin to prevent the sides from overcooking.

2 Remove any stalks from the fruit. Place in a bowl and pour over the sherry, brandy or juice. Stir well.

3 Add the cherries, mixed peel, grated rind, chopped almonds and ground almonds.

4 Add the mixed spice, nutmeg and salt to the flour and sieve into a bowl.

5 Crack the eggs into a basin and beat lightly.

6 Cream the fat and sugar together until light and fluffy. Beat in the black treacle and gradually add the eggs, beating well between each addition. If the mixture begins to curdle, sieve in a little flour.

7 Fold in the sieved flour, mixed spice and nutmeg. Fold in the fruit, cherries, mixed peel, grated rind and nuts until thoroughly mixed.

8 Spoon into the tin, level out and bake.

9 Test with a skewer. It should come out clean if the cake is cooked; if not, test at 15 minute intervals.

10 When cooked, remove from the oven and allow to cool in the tin for a while, then turn out on to a wire rack. Remove the grease-proof paper and allow to cool thoroughly before wrapping in fresh greaseproof paper and foil and placing in an airtight tin or box. Store for 2–3 months before covering with almond paste and icing.

TEMP	TIME
120–130°C (no need to preheat)	$2^{1}/_{2}$–$3^{1}/_{4}$ hours for the smaller cake 3–$3^{1}/_{2}$ hours for the larger cake

COOK'S NOTE

During storage, prick the cake with a skewer occasionally and brush the surface with brandy or sherry to keep the cake moist.

Alternative cooking method if available:

Suggested temp:130–140°C or equivalent (preheat for 10–15 minutes)
Time: as in recipe above

NB: Only one shelf level at a time should be used on this function.

RASPBERRY BUNS

MAKES 12

※

75 g/3 oz/^{1}/$_3$ cup block margarine
225 g/8 oz/2 cups self-raising (self-rising) flour
Salt
75 g/3 oz/^{1}/$_3$ cup caster (superfine) sugar
2 eggs, beaten
30 ml/2 tbsp raspberry jam (conserve)

1 Rub the fat into the flour until the mixture resembles fine breadcrumbs.

2 Add the salt and sugar and mix to a stiff dough with the eggs.

3 Turn on to a floured board, knead lightly and divide into 12 pieces.

4 Flour your hands and shape the pieces into balls. Place on a sheet of greaseproof (waxed) paper on a baking tray, leaving room for expansion. Flour your finger and make a deep hole in the centre of each bun. Put 2.5 ml/^{1}/$_2$ tsp jam in each hole.

5 Bake.

TEMP	TIME
170°C	20 minutes (if preheated) OR 25 minutes (from cold)

YORKSHIRE PARKIN

MAKES 20 SQUARES

✳

225 g/8 oz/1 cup margarine
225 g/8 oz/²/₃ cup golden (light corn) syrup
50 g/2 oz/1 tbsp black treacle
225 g/8 oz/2 cups self-raising (self-rising) flour
225 g/8 oz/2 cups medium oatmeal
225 g/8 oz/1 cup demerara (light brown) sugar
15 ml/1 tbsp ground ginger
300 ml/¹/₂ pt/1¹/₄ cups milk
1 egg, beaten

1 Grease and line a 25–30 cm (10–12 in) square cake tin.

2 Melt the margarine, syrup and black treacle together and allow to cool a little.

3 Mix the dry ingredients together, add the melted ingredients and stir in the milk and egg.

4 Pour mixture into the tin and spread gently.

5 Bake.

TEMP	TIME
140°C (no need to preheat)	1¹/₂–2 hours (depending on depth of tin)

COOK'S NOTE
Parkin tastes better if cut into squares and kept in a tin for a few days to a week.

MUNCH
(A kind of flapjack)

MAKES 12–15 SQUARES

✳

30 ml/2 tbsp golden (light corn) syrup
100 g/4 oz/¹/₂ cup margarine
15 ml/1 tbsp water
225 g/8 oz/2 cups rolled oats
175 g/6 oz/1¹/₂ cups self-raising (self-rising) flour
100 g/4 oz/¹/₂ cup caster (superfine) sugar
2.5 ml/¹/₂ tsp bicarbonate of soda (baking soda)

1 Grease a baking tin (pan) approximately 30 × 23 cm (12 × 9 in).

2 Put the syrup, margarine and water into a saucepan and heat gently until melted.

3 Add the liquid to the dry ingredients and stir until thoroughly combined into a soft dough.

4 Spread the mixture into the tin.

5 Bake until firm to the touch and lightly golden. Allow to cool in the tin, cut into squares and store in an airtight container.

TEMP	TIME
160°C	25 minutes (from cold) OR 20 minutes (if preheated)

COOK'S NOTE
Munch is best left for 2–3 days before eating and can be kept for a few weeks.

CINNAMON BISCUITS

COURTESY OF SCHOLTES UK

MAKES 30

❋

100 g/4 oz/^{1}/$_2$ cup butter

225 g/8 oz/2 cups plain (all-purpose) flour

2.5 ml/^{1}/$_2$ tsp baking powder

150 g/5 oz/^{2}/$_3$ cup brown sugar

15 ml/1 tbsp ground cinnamon

1 egg

1 Cream the butter in a large bowl.

2 Sift the flour and baking powder on to the butter and add the sugar, cinnamon and egg. Mix the ingredients together well.

3 Gather the dough into a ball.

4 Roll out to a thickness of 5 mm (^{1}/$_4$ in). Cut into shapes using biscuit cutters. Place on trays lined with non-stick baking parchment.

5 Bake.

TEMP	TIME
170°C (preheated for 5–8 minutes)	15–20 minutes

COOK'S NOTE
Mixed spice can be used instead of cinnamon. This makes a tasty Christmas biscuit, especially if you use seasonal cutters, such as holly leaves or stars.

EASTER BISCUITS

MAKES 24

✳

75 g/3 oz/^{1}/$_3$ cup butter
60 g/2^1/$_2$ oz/^{1}/$_4$ cup caster (superfine) sugar
1 egg, separated
175 g/6 oz/1^1/$_2$ cups self-raising (self-rising) flour
Salt
2.5 ml/^{1}/$_2$ tsp mixed (apple-pie) spice
40 g/1^1/$_2$ oz/^{1}/$_4$ cup currants
10 g/^{1}/$_2$ oz/^{1}/$_2$ tbsp mixed peel (optional)
15–30 ml/1–2 tbsp milk
Caster (superfine) sugar, for dredging

1 Grease two baking sheets or line with baking parchment.

2 Cream the butter and sugar and beat in the egg yolk.

3 Sieve the flour, salt and mixed spice into the creamed mixture and fold in. Gently stir in the fruit and mixed peel.

4 Add enough milk to form a soft dough, knead gently and roll out to about 3 mm (^{1}/$_8$ in) thick. Cut into rounds using a 6 cm (2^1/$_2$ in) fluted cutter dipped in flour. Place on baking trays.

5 Bake for half the cooking time, brush with slightly beaten egg white and sprinkle with a little caster sugar. Bake again.

TEMP	TIME
170°C (no need to preheat)	10 minutes, then a further 10 minutes with sugar

SHREWSBURY BISCUITS

MAKES 24

✳

100 g/4 oz/¹/₂ cup butter

225 g/8 oz/2 cups plain (all-purpose) flour

100 g/4 oz/¹/₂ cup caster (superfine) sugar

1 egg, beaten

Grated rind of 1 lemon

1 Rub the butter into the flour until the mixture resembles fine breadcrumbs.

2 Add the sugar, egg and lemon rind and form a firm dough.

3 Knead lightly until smooth and roll out on a lightly floured board to 5 mm (¹/₄ in) thick. Cut out with a 5 cm (2 in) fluted cutter.

4 Put on trays lined with baking parchment, prick with a fork. Bake.

TEMP	TIME
160°C	15-20 minutes (if preheated) 20-25 minutes (from cold)

COOK'S NOTES

Novelty shapes can be used for children, and flavours varied as follows:

Add 10 ml/2 tsp mixed (apple-pie) spice or cinnamon

OR 5 ml/1 level tsp vanilla essence (extract)

OR 50 g/2 oz/¹/₃ cup dried fruit or chopped glacé (candied) cherries.

SHORTBREAD

MAKES 1 LARGE ROUND OR 12 BISCUITS

✳

100 g/4 oz/$^1/_2$ cup butter, softened
50 g/2 oz/$^1/_4$ cup caster (superfine) sugar
150 g/5 oz/$1^1/_4$ cups plain (all-purpose) flour
Salt
25 g/1 oz/2 tbsp ground rice
Caster (superfine) sugar, for dredging

1 Cream the butter and half the sugar, work in the flour, salt and ground rice, then the remaining sugar.

2 Knead well on a floured board until free from cracks. Press and shape into a round on a baking sheet and prick lightly with a fork. Crimp the edges with a fork. Bake.

3 Mark into portions with a knife while warm. Dredge with caster sugar when cool. Store in an airtight container.

TEMP	TIME
140°C	40 minutes (if preheated) OR 45 minutes (from cold)
COOK'S NOTE	
If preferred, roll thinly and cut into rounds with a fluted pastry cutter and bake as follows: Temperature: 165°C Time: 20 minutes (if preheated) 25 minutes (from cold).	

ROCK CAKES

MAKES 8

✳

150 g/5 oz/²/₃ cup block margarine

225 g/8 oz/2 cups self-raising (self-rising) flour, sifted

75 g/3 oz/¹/₃ cup demerara (light brown) sugar

2.5 ml/¹/₂ tsp mixed ground (apple-pie) spice

150 g/5 oz/³/₄ cup mixed dried fruit (fruit cake mix)

1 egg, lightly beaten

30 ml/2 tbsp milk

1 Line two baking sheets with baking parchment (or grease lightly).

2 Rub the margarine into the flour until the mixture resembles fine breadcrumbs (a food processor can be used for this).

3 Stir in the sugar, spice and fruit then mix in the egg and milk to make a fairly stiff mixture.

4 Place 8 spoonfuls of the mixture, well spaced, on to the baking sheets.

5 Bake. Cool on a wire rack.

TEMP	TIME
175°C	20 minutes (if preheated) OR 25 minutes (from cold)

WHITE BREAD DOUGH

USE TO MAKE 2 LOAVES OR 36 SMALL ROLLS

1.5 kg/3 lb/12 cups strong white (bread) flour
15 ml/1 tbsp salt
50 g/2 oz/¹/₄ cup lard OR block margarine
2 sachets easy-blend yeast
900 ml/1¹/₂ pt/3³/₄ cups (approx.) warm water

1 Sieve the flour and salt into a large warmed mixing bowl. Rub in the fat and stir in the yeast.

2 Stir in the warm water and mix to a soft dough.

3 Turn on to a floured board and knead thoroughly for 10 minutes until smooth.

4 Shape the dough to use in one of the suggested ways, cover with oiled clingfilm (plastic wrap) and allow to prove until doubled in size.

NB: If adapting your own bread recipe, 15 g/¹/₂ oz/1 tbsp easy-blend yeast is the equivalent of 25 g/1 oz/2 tbsp fresh yeast. Dough made with fresh yeast will need proving then knocking back before shaping.

TIN LOAVES

1 Grease 2 × 900 g (2 lb) loaf tins.

2 Split the dough in half and shape each half to fit the base of a tin. Cover with oiled clingfilm (plastic wrap) and prove for 30–40 minutes.

3 Make two small slits across the top of the dough and bake.

TEMP	TIME
200–210°C (preheated for 8 minutes)	30–40 minutes

COOK'S NOTE
To get the temperature of the warm water right, use one part boiling to two parts cold.

COTTAGE LOAVES

MAKES 2

1 Grease a baking tray. Halve the dough.

2 Cut one-third off each piece and shape this and the remaining two-thirds into two pairs of balls, one large and one small.

3 Press a slight dip in each large ball and place them on the baking sheet. Place the small balls on top.

4 Cover with oiled clingfilm (plastic wrap) and leave to prove for about 30 minutes. Bake.

TEMP	TIME
200–210°C (preheat for 8 minutes)	30–40 minutes

PLAIT

MAKES 2

1 Divide the dough into six equal pieces.

2 Roll each into a sausage shape 30–40 cm (12–16 in). Lay these next to each other on a greased or lined baking tray.

3 Press the top ends of three pieces together and tuck under, then loosely plait all the way down, pinching and tucking the other ends together. Repeat for the other three pieces.

4 Cover with oiled clingfilm (plastic wrap) and leave to prove for about 30 minutes.

5 Brush with a little milk and sprinkle with poppy seeds if liked. Bake.

TEMP	TIME
200–210°C (preheat for 8 minutes)	30–40 minutes

ROLLS

MAKES 20–22

1 Use half the quantity of dough and divide into 20–22 equal portions.

2 Shape into balls or mini-plaits or finger rolls and place on greased or lined baking trays, well spaced.

3 Cover with oiled clingfilm (plastic wrap) and leave to rise for 30–40 minutes until doubled in size.

4 Brush with beaten egg or dust with flour for a softer finish. Bake.

TEMP	TIME
200–210°C (preheat for 8 minutes)	20–25 minutes

COOK'S NOTE
The white bread can be given additional flavourings when adding the flour. Make half the quantity and add 225 g /8 oz/2 cups grated Cheddar cheese and/or 25 g/1 oz/2 tbsp caraway seeds or 10 ml/2 tsp freshly chopped herbs.

WHOLEMEAL BREAD

MAKES 2 LOAVES OR 36 ROLLS

❊

1.5 kg/3 lb/12 cups wholemeal flour

15 ml/1 tbsp salt

50 g/2 oz/¹/₄ cup lard

2 sachets easy-blend yeast

1 Make as for White Bread Dough (see page 107) and after kneading shape into loaves, rolls or a rough circle on a baking tin with a cross cut on the top to divide the loaf into quarters.

2 Bake as for white bread.

TEMP	TIME
200°C (preheat for 8 minutes)	25–30 minutes (rolls) 35–40 minutes (loaves)
COOK'S NOTE	
For a lighter wholemeal bread use 4 cups wholemeal flour and 2 cups strong white flour.	

CHEESE AND ONION BREAD

COURTESY OF ZANUSSI LTD

MAKES 2

✳

½ quantity white bread dough (see page 107)

For the filling:
100 g/4 oz/1 cup grated cheese
1 medium onion, finely chopped

1 Turn the dough on to a lightly floured surface, divide into two and roll each piece out to a rectangular shape. Spread the grated cheese and onion over each rectangle and roll up tightly from the narrow end like a Swiss (jelly) roll.

2 Place each roll in a 450 g (1 lb) loaf tin and leave to prove for 30 minutes. Bake until the loaves shrink in the tins or sound hollow

TEMP	TIME
200°C (preheat for 8 minutes)	25–30 minutes

Savoury Dishes

Stuffed Courgettes

SERVES 4

❋

4 courgettes (zucchini)
1 small onion, finely chopped
225 g/7 oz/1 small can chopped tomatoes, drained
5 ml/1 tsp chopped fresh parsley
OR 2.5 ml/$^1/_2$ tsp dried parsley
Dash of Worcestershire sauce
Salt and freshly ground black pepper
25 g/1 oz/2 tbsp butter
50 g/2 oz/1 cup fresh breadcrumbs
50 g/2 oz/$^1/_2$ cup Parmesan cheese, grated

1 Cut the courgettes in half lengthways and scoop out the flesh.

2 Roughly chop the flesh of the courgettes, mix with the chopped onion, tomatoes, parsley, Worcestershire sauce and seasoning. Melt the butter in a frying pan and cook the mixture gently until soft. Stir in the breadcrumbs.

3 Fill the courgettes with the mixture and sprinkle with cheese.

4 Place on a solid baking sheet and bake. Serve immediately.

TEMP	TIME
170–180°C	25 minutes (if preheated) 30 minutes (from cold)

STUFFED PEPPERS

SERVES 6

✳

6 red or yellow (bell) peppers
50 g/2 oz/1 cup mushrooms
175 g/6 oz/³/₄ cup pesto sauce
75 g/3 oz/1¹/₂ cups fresh breadcrumbs
Salt and freshly ground black pepper
15 ml/1 tbsp tomato purée (paste)
15 ml/1 tbsp soy sauce
2 plum tomatoes
Olive oil, for brushing

1 Cut the peppers in half lengthways, leaving the stalk on for a more attractive appearance when cooked.

2 Carefully remove the centre core and the seeds with a sharp knife. Wash the pepper halves.

3 Chop the mushrooms finely and mix with all the other ingredients except the tomatoes and oil.

4 Share the mixture evenly among the peppers, pressing down lightly.

5 Place a slice of tomato on top of each pepper. Brush the exposed edges of pepper with a little olive oil.

6 Cook in a shallow ovenproof dish.

TEMP	TIME
170–180°C	30–40 minutes (from cold OR preheated: timing is not critical)
COOK'S NOTE	
Can be assembled the day before. Can stay in the hot oven for a further 30 minutes if necessary without spoiling.	

RATATOUILLE

SERVES 6–8

✳

30 ml/2 tbsp olive oil OR corn oil
50 g/2 oz/$^1/_4$ cup butter
1 large onion, sliced
1 garlic clove, crushed
2 aubergines (eggplant)
225 g/8 oz/1 cup courgettes, (zucchini), sliced
1 red (bell) pepper, sliced
1 green (bell) pepper, sliced
300 ml/$^1/_2$ pt/2 cups passata (sieved tomatoes)
5 tomatoes, skinned and sliced
Salt and freshly ground black pepper
5 ml/1 tsp oregano
10 ml/2 tsp chopped fresh parsley
Dash of Worcestershire sauce
30 ml/2 tbsp tomato purée (paste)

1 Sprinkle the aubergines with salt and leave for 30 minutes. Rinse, drain thoroughly and dry on kitchen paper.

2 Heat 1 tbsp oil with the butter in a frying pan and gently fry the onion and garlic until the onion is beginning to soften.

3 Remove with a slotted spoon and transfer to an ovenproof casserole (Dutch oven).

4 Brown the aubergine slices in the hot pan, a few at a time. Add more of the oil if necessary.

5 Add the aubergines to the casserole along with all the other ingredients and seasoning.

6 Stir gently, cover with a lid or foil and bake in the oven. Stir once during cooking.

TEMP	TIME
160°C (preheat for 5–8 minutes as some ingredients are warm)	60–70 minutes

COOK'S NOTE
To skin tomatoes, cut a cross in the base of each tomato and cover with boiling water for 30 seconds. Peel off the loosened skin.

CHEESEY STUFFED TOMATOES

SERVES 8 AS A STARTER OR AN ACCOMPANIMENT TO A MAIN COURSE

❋

4 large beef tomatoes

1 onion

75 g/3 oz/1¹/₂ cups fresh breadcrumbs

50 g/2 oz/1 cup button mushrooms, sliced

10 ml/2 tsp chopped fresh parsley

Salt and freshly ground black pepper

75 g/3 oz/³/₄ cup Gruyère (Swiss) OR strong Cheddar cheese, grated

1 Cut each tomato in half and scoop out the centre, discarding the hard core but saving the juice and seeds.

2 Chop the onion finely and mix with the breadcrumbs, mushrooms, herbs, seasoning and enough of the juice from the tomatoes to bind the mixture together.

3 Sprinkle the cheese on top of each tomato. Place in a shallow ovenproof dish and bake.

TEMP	TIME
170–180°C (no need to preheat)	30 minutes

GRUYERE-TOPPED POTATO BAKE

SERVES 4–6

✳

4 large potatoes, peeled and thinly sliced
1 large Spanish onion, thinly sliced
425 ml/³/₄ pt/2 cups chicken stock
Salt and freshly ground black pepper
50 g/2 oz/¹/₂ cup Gruyère (Swiss) cheese, grated
25 g/1 oz/¹/₄ cup Cheddar cheese, grated

1 Place alternate layers of potato and onion in a buttered ovenproof dish at least 7.5 cm (3 in) deep. Season each layer.

2 Pour over the stock. Cover with clingfilm (plastic wrap) and microwave on high for 20 minutes.

3 Uncover and sprinkle the cheeses over the top. Bake.

TEMP	TIME
190°C (preheat for 5–8 minutes)	30–40 minutes (until top is a golden brown and the potatoes are soft)

Additional cooking functions if available (refer to your manufacturer's instructions for guidance):

OR

Suggested temp: 180–190°C or equivalent
Time: for the last 15 minutes of cooking if the topping requires extra browning.

BAKED POTATOES

SERVES 4

※

4 × 225 g/8 oz baking potatoes

For the toppings:
50 g/2 oz/¹/₂ cup strong Cheddar cheese, grated
OR **75 g/3 oz/³/₄ cup baked beans**
OR **75 g/3 oz/¹/₃ cup cottage cheese**
OR **175 g/6 oz/1¹/₂ cups peeled prawns (shrimp) mixed with**
45 ml(3 tbsp) mayonnaise
OR **100 g/4 oz/¹/₂ cup butter**
Salt and freshly ground black pepper

1 Scrub the potatoes, pierce the skin with a fork and bake.

2 While the potatoes are cooking prepare the topping of your choice.

3 When the potatoes are cooked, make a cross in the top of each and squeeze open.

4 Spoon the topping equally between the potatoes and season.

NB: If preferred add 10 g/¹/₂ oz/1 tbsp butter or low-fat spread on top of each potato before adding the topping.

TEMP	TIME
175°C (no need to preheat)	1¹/₂ hours
COOK'S NOTE	
To reduce the cooking time, you could begin cooking the potatoes in a microwave until almost soft, then finish in the oven for the last 20 minutes.	

BRAZIL NUT BAKE

COURTESY OF DE DIETRICH

SERVES 4–6

✳

15 ml/1 tbsp oil
1 onion, finely chopped
100 g/4 oz/1 cup Brazil nuts, roughly chopped
100 g/4 oz/1 cup peanuts, roughly chopped
175 g/6 oz/3 cups fresh wholemeal breadcrumbs
6 tomatoes, skinned and roughly chopped
200 ml/7 fl oz/1 cup tomato juice
15 ml/1 tbsp dried mixed herbs
Dash of Worcestershire sauce
Salt and freshly ground black pepper

1 Heat the oil in a saucepan and gently fry the onion until softened. Remove from the heat and stir in the remaining ingredients.

2 Press into a greased 900 g(2 lb) loaf tin and cook.

3 Leave in the tin for 10 minutes before turning out and serving.

TEMP	TIME
170°C (no need to preheat)	40–45 minutes or until firm and lightly browned

CHEESE AND BACON STUFFED POTATO

SERVES 4

✳

4 × 225 g/8 oz baking potatoes
4 streaky bacon rashers (slices)
100 g/4 oz/1 cup strong Cheddar cheese, grated
Salt and freshly ground black pepper
25 g/1 oz/2 tbsp butter OR low-fat spread

1 Scrub the potatoes, slit the skin with a sharp knife in a circle around the length of the potato and bake.

TEMP	TIME
175°C	1¹/₂ hours

2 While cooking, prepare the filling. Cook the bacon (grill, microwave or dry fry) and cut into small pieces. Allow to cool and mix with two-thirds of the cheese in a bowl.

3 Cut the baked potatoes in half. Scoop out the centre and mix with the bacon and cheese.

4 Add the seasoning to taste and the butter or low-fat spread. Mix well with a fork.

⑤ Divide the filling among the potato skins. Sprinkle the remaining cheese over the top and return to the oven until the cheese has melted and browned on top.

TEMP	TIME
180°C (preheat for 5–8 minutes)	10–15 minutes

COOK'S NOTE
The potatoes can be prepared and filled the day before then baked for 30–35 minutes until heated through thoroughly. Vary the filling by adding Gruyère cheese instead of Cheddar, or using tuna, ham, salami, etc. instead of the bacon.

Alternative cooking function if available (refer to your manufacturer's instructions for guidance):

 Suggested temp: 160–170°C or equivalent (preheated for 5 minutes)
Time: 15 minutes OR for the last 15 minutes of cooking if the potatoes have been prepared earlier

BRAISED RED CABBAGE

COURTESY OF TRICITY BENDIX

SERVES 6–8

✳

50 g/2 oz/^{1}/$_4$ cup butter
900 g/2 lb/8 cups red cabbage, finely shredded
2 onions, sliced
2 garlic cloves, finely chopped
2 cooking (tart) apples, diced
1 bay leaf
2.5 ml/^{1}/$_2$ tsp chopped fresh parsley
Pinch of dried thyme
Pinch of ground cinnamon
Pinch of ground nutmeg
Salt and freshly ground black pepper
Grated rind of 1 orange
5 ml/1 tsp caraway seeds
15 ml/1 tbsp brown sugar
1 small glass red wine

1 Place all the ingredients in a casserole dish (Dutch oven). Stir well.

2 Cover with a well-fitting lid (a layer of greaseproof paper under the lid helps). Bake. Stir twice during cooking.

TEMP	TIME
150°C (from cold)	2–2^1/$_2$ hours

COOK'S NOTE
Once cooked and cooled this dish freezes well or it can be cooked 2–3 days in advance and reheated.

VEGETABLE CASSEROLE

COURTESY OF BELLING LTD

SERVES 4

2 large potatoes, washed and sliced, skins on

2 carrots, sliced

$^1/_2$ medium swede (rutabaga), diced

2 leeks, sliced

Salt and freshly ground black pepper

150 ml/$^1/_4$ pt/$^2/_3$ cup vegetable stock

5 ml/1 tsp oregano

50 g/2 oz/1 cup fresh brown or white breadcrumbs

50 g/2 oz/$^1/_2$ cup mature Cheddar cheese, grated

1 Grease a 1.5 litre (2$^1/_4$ pt) ovenproof casserole (Dutch oven).

2 Arrange the vegetables in layers in the casserole, beginning and ending with a layer of potatoes. Season between each layer.

3 Pour the stock over the vegetables. Cover with a tight-fitting lid or foil and cook.

TEMP	TIME
160°C (no need to preheat)	1$^1/_2$–2 hours

4 Remove lid. Sprinkle cheese and breadcrumbs on top of the casserole. Return to oven uncovered and cook.

TEMP	TIME
170°C (already hot)	10–15 minutes

STUFFED MARROW

SERVES 4–6

✳

1 marrow (squash)

For the meat sauce:
225 g/8 oz/2 cups minced (ground) meat
1 onion, finely chopped
1 carrot, grated
45 ml/3 tbsp tomato purée (paste)
5 ml/1 tsp oregano OR dried mixed herbs
2 garlic cloves, crushed
150 ml/¹/₄ pt/²/₃ cup water
50 g/2 oz/1 cup mushrooms
Salt and freshly ground black pepper
Dash of Worcestershire sauce

For the tomato sauce:
1 small onion, chopped
1 garlic clove, crushed
300 ml/¹/₂ pt/1¹/₄ cups passata (sieved tomatoes)
10 ml/2 tsp olive oil
Salt and freshly ground black pepper
Dash of Worcestershire sauce
Pinch of oregano

1 Combine all the meat sauce ingredients in a saucepan and simmer with a lid on for 30–40 minutes until the meat is well cooked.

2 Skim any excess fat from the top and discard.

3 Adjust the seasoning.

4 Slice the marrow into 6 cm (2¹/₂ in) rings.

5 Remove the centre core and seeds. Peel strips of the skin away. Arrange the marrow rings in a shallow dish.

6 Fill with the meat sauce, cover with foil and bake.

7 For the tomato sauce, fry the onion until soft, add the garlic and cook for 2–3 more minutes.

8 Add the other sauce ingredients and heat gently.

9 Serve sauce separately with the baked stuffed marrow.

TEMP	TIME
170°C (no need to preheat)	60 minutes

CHEESE SOUFFLE

SERVES 4

※

50 g/2 oz/^{1}/$_2$ cup Cheddar cheese, grated
50 g/2 oz/^{1}/$_2$ cup Gruyère (Swiss) cheese, grated
40 g/1^1/$_2$ oz/3 tbsp butter
25 g/1 oz/^{1}/$_4$ cup plain (all-purpose) flour
300 ml/^{1}/$_2$ pt/1^1/$_4$ cups milk
Salt and freshly ground black pepper
Pinch of grated nutmeg
4 egg yolks
5 ml/1 tsp made mustard
6 egg whites

1 Grease a 1.2 litre (2 pt) soufflé dish.

2 Mix together the two cheeses.

3 Melt the butter in a saucepan, stir in the flour. Remove the pan from the heat and gradually stir in the milk. Replace on the heat and bring the sauce to the boil, stirring all the time. Season and add the nutmeg.

4 Simmer for 2 minutes, then remove from the heat and beat the egg yolks into the hot sauce. Allow to cool slightly, stir in the mustard and three-quarters of the mixed cheeses, and adjust seasoning.

5 Whisk the egg whites until stiff. Stir in about a quarter of the egg whites to the still hot sauce. Add this to the rest of the egg whites and fold in as lightly as possible with a metal spoon.

6 Pour the mixture into the dish and smooth the surface. Sprinkle with the remaining cheese and bake.

TEMP	TIME
190–200°C (preheat for 8 minutes)	15 20 minutes

COOK'S NOTE

The soufflé can be prepared 3–4 hours in advance up to and including stage 4. Cover the surface with a piece of buttered greaseproof (waxed) paper. Heat the cheese mixture until hot to the touch before adding the egg whites.

BAKED STUFFED TROUT

SERVES 4

❋

4 trout
Lemon juice, to taste
2.5 ml/¹/₂ tsp chopped fresh parsley
Pinch of dill (dill weed)
Pinch of tarragon
2.5 ml/¹/₂ tsp rosemary
50 g/2 oz/¹/₄ cup butter, softened
100 g/4 oz/1 cup prawns (shrimp), drained and dried
Salt and freshly ground black pepper
Oil, for brushing

1 Remove the heads and bones from the trout and sprinkle the inside with lemon juice.

2 Cream the herbs, salt and pepper into the butter, lightly mix in the prawns and spread inside the trout.

3 Lay the trout on a baking tray lined with baking parchment, brush with oil and cook.

TEMP	TIME
180°C	25–30 minutes (if preheated) OR 30–35 minutes (from cold)

COOK'S NOTE
To bone the fish, place backbone uppermost and press along the length of the backbone until it gives. Turn over and gently prise it out along with the other bones.

CRUNCHY-TOPPED FISH BAKE

COURTESY OF ATAG (UK) LTD

SERVES 4

❋

4 plaice fillets, skinned
OR 350 g/12 oz cod fillet, boned and skinned
1 × 300 ml/10 oz medium can condensed mushroom soup
100 g/4 oz/1 cup grated cheese
50 g/2 oz/¼ cup butter
5 ml/1 tsp grated onion
Dash of Worcestershire sauce
Pinch of garlic salt
1 small bag plain crisps (potato chips), crushed
Anchovies (optional)

① Place the fillets in a greased ovenproof dish. Pour over the soup and top with the cheese.

② Melt the butter, add the onion, Worcestershire sauce and garlic salt. Mix well.

③ Add the crushed crisps and mix again. Spread the mixture over the fish and bake.

④ Garnish with a criss-cross of anchovies if wished.

TEMP	TIME
150°C	30 minutes (if preheated) OR 35 minutes (from cold)

SMOKED HADDOCK QUICHE

SERVES 4–6

✳

175 g/6 oz shortcrust pastry (basic pie dough)
225 g/8 oz smoked haddock
Milk, for steaming
2 eggs
1 egg yolk
120 g/4 fl oz/^{1}/$_2$ cup single (light) cream
OR 1 small can condensed milk
50 g/2 oz/^{1}/$_2$ cup sweetcorn (corn)
Salt and freshly ground black pepper
50 g/2 oz/^{1}/$_2$ cup cheese, grated

1 Roll out the pastry and use to line a 20 cm (8 in) flan tin (pie shell). Prick the base lightly with a fork.

2 Bake blind.

3 While pastry is cooking, steam the haddock in a little milk and black pepper until just cooked (microwaving is ideal for this).

4 Flake the fish on to a clean plate, discarding the skin and bones.

5 Beat the eggs and yolk in a bowl. Add the fish, cream and sweetcorn.

6 Season (sparingly) and pour into the flan case. Sprinkle with the cheese.

7 Bake in the already hot oven until the top is set and golden.

TEMP	TIME
170–180°C	30–40 minutes

Additional cooking functions if available (refer to your manufacturer's instructions for guidance):

   OR

Suggested temp: 190°C (preheat for 8 minutes)
Time: 20 minutes
THEN 170–180°C
Time: 25–30 minutes

NB: There is no need to bake the pastry first with these functions.

SALMON IN PUFF PASTRY

COURTESY OF GAGGENAU (UK) LTD

SERVES 6

✳

450 g/1 lb puff pastry (paste)
750 g/1¹/₂ lb boned skinless fresh salmon
100 g/4 oz cucumber
Beaten egg, for glazing

For the sauce:
25 g/1 oz/2 tbsp plain (all-purpose) flour
25 g/1 oz/2 tbsp butter
150 ml/¹/₄ pt/²/₃ cup milk
150 ml/¹/₄ pt/²/₃ cup double (heavy) cream
Salt and white pepper
2.5 ml/¹/₂ tsp dill (dill weed)

1 Make a roux with the butter and flour (i.e. melt the butter in the pan then stir in the flour). Do not let it brown at all. Mix the milk and cream together and add it to the roux gradually, off the heat, until all the liquid is mixed smoothly. Return to the heat, stirring all the time, until the sauce thickens.

2 Season to taste, then add the dill weed. Then cover the surface with a little melted butter or a piece of buttered greaseproof (waxed) paper to prevent a skin forming. Allow to cool.

3 Cut the salmon into 2.5 cm (1 in) cubes and mix into the sauce.

4 Roll the pastry out into a rectangle approximately 30 × 38 cm (12 × 15in). Place on a baking tray lined with baking parchment or silicone paper. Make slight impressions lengthways on the pastry to divide it into three equal sections, without cutting through.

Make diagonal cuts about 2.5 cm (1 in) apart down both sides of each strip. Roll out rectangle of pastry and cut edges as shown (1). Lay filling down the centre (2).

  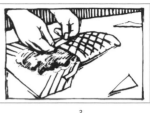

1.   2.   3.

5 Slice the cucumber thinly and arrange the slices to cover the centre strip. Spread the salmon mixture over the cucumber.

6 Moisten the outer strips with water. Fold over the top end of the pastry, then fold the cut strips alternately side by side over the salmon until it is totally enclosed and looks like a plait (3). Tuck the bottom end under the last few strips.

7 Brush with beaten egg and bake.

TEMP	TIME
190–200°C (preheat for 5-8 minutes)	45 minutes

COOK'S NOTES
If extra dill sauce is required make double the quantity and reserve half to be reheated later. The filling can be varied by using part salmon and part white fish or prawns (shrimp).

Additional cooking functions if available (refer to your manufacturer's instructions for guidance):

OR

Suggested temp: 190°C or equivalent
Time: for the last 20 minutes of cooking

WHOLE POACHED SALMON

SERVES 12–15 AS A BUFFET ITEM, OR 6–8 AS A MAIN COURSE

✳

1.5 kg/3¹/₄ lb minimum whole salmon OR sea trout
Melted butter, for greasing
¹/₂ cucumber, sliced paper thin
1 olive
300 ml/¹/₂ pt/1¹/₄ cups aspic jelly
Parsley, watercress OR red lettuce, to garnish

For the cooking liquid:
150 ml/¹/₄ pt/²/₃ cup wine vinegar OR wine
1 onion, quartered
1 carrot, cut in chunks
1 celery stalk, sliced
3 bay leaves
15 ml/1 tbsp lemon juice
900 ml/1¹/₂ pt/3³/₄ cups water
A few peppercorns
5 ml/1 tsp dried thyme
A few parsley stems
1 garlic clove, crushed

1 Put all the ingredients for the cooking liquid in a saucepan, bring to the boil and simmer for 30 minutes. Strain and allow to cool.

2 Clean and wipe the fish, leaving the head on; rub salt inside along the backbone to remove any blood. Open gill flaps and snip out the feathery red gills.

3 Place fish in a greased roasting tin. If the head does not fit cut it off but cook it with the salmon; it can be replaced later and the join concealed with parsley.

④ Fold strips of foil and position under the salmon at intervals for lifting out once cooked. Pour in the cooking liquid.

⑤ Grease a sheet of foil with melted butter and cover the fish. Seal the edges well but try to avoid touching the fish with the foil.

⑥ Bake. Lift out on to a grid and allow to cool and drain, leaving the foil straps in place.

⑦ Lift the salmon on to a serving dish and remove the foil straps.

⑧ Cut through the skin along the backbone and peel the skin away from one side. Turn over and skin the other side. Scrape away the brown flesh gently to reveal the pink flesh underneath.

⑨ When completely cold, decorate with cucumber slices, overlapping around the head and tail to give the appearance of scales. Put half the olive over the eye.

⑩ Make up the aspic, cool until just beginning to set, then spoon over the fish and cucumber.

⑪ Finally, garnish with parsley, watercress or red lettuce and serve with mayonnaise and salads.

TEMP	TIME
160–170°C (no need to preheat)	10 minutes per 450 g/1 lb

COOK'S NOTE

The fish can be served hot: lift on to a warm serving dish and skin as soon as the salmon has drained. There is no need to remove the brown flesh. Serve with fresh vegetables and hollandaise sauce.

CHICKEN CURRY

COURTESY OF IMPERIAL (UK) LTD

SERVES 4

❋

4 chicken breasts, cut into pieces
30 ml/2 tbsp oil
1 onion, finely chopped
1 garlic clove, crushed
5 ml/1 tsp garam masala
5 ml/1 tsp ground cumin
2.5 ml/^{1}/$_2$ tsp ground cinnamon
2.5 ml/^{1}/$_2$ tsp mixed (apple-pie) spice
2.5 ml/^{1}/$_2$ tsp chilli powder
2.5 ml/^{1}/$_2$ tsp turmeric
10 ml/2 tsp curry powder
5 ml/1 tsp freshly grated ginger
50 g/2 oz/^{1}/$_2$ cup creamed coconut
50 g/2 oz/^{1}/$_3$ cup sultanas (golden raisins)
50 g/2 oz/^{1}/$_2$ cup ground almonds
150 ml/^{1}/$_4$ pt/^{2}/$_3$ cup water
60 ml/4 tbsp cream

1 Fry the chicken in the oil and transfer to a casserole (Dutch oven).

2 Fry the onion until soft, add the garlic and fry for 2 minutes.

3 Add all the spices and ginger, mix well and cook for a further 2 minutes. Add the creamed coconut, sultanas, ground almonds and water, mix well and simmer for 5 minutes to allow the flavours to blend.

4 Transfer to the casserole, mix with the chicken, cover and cook.

5 Add the cream for the last 20 minutes of cooking time.

TEMP	TIME
160°C (no need to preheat)	1 hour

CHICKEN WITH PEPPERS

SERVES 4

✳

4 chicken joints, skinned
1 red (bell) pepper, sliced
1 onion, thinly sliced
300 ml/^{1}/$_2$ pt/1^1/$_4$ cups chicken stock
300 ml/^{1}/$_2$ pt/1^1/$_4$ cups passata (sieved tomatoes)
OR 225 g/7 oz/1 small can chopped tomatoes
15 ml/1 tbsp white wine
5 ml/1 tsp oregano
15 ml/1 tbsp soy sauce
Salt and freshly ground black pepper

1 Place the chicken in an ovenproof casserole dish (Dutch oven) and sprinkle the peppers and onion over the top.

2 Mix the stock, passata, white wine, oregano, soy sauce and seasoning together and pour over the chicken. Cover with a lid or foil.

3 Bake.

TEMP	TIME
180°C (no need to preheat)	1 hour

VEAL WITH PAPRIKA

COURTESY OF MIELE LTD

SERVES 4

❊

4 streaky bacon rasher (slices)
25 g/1 oz/2 tbsp butter
2 onions, sliced
750 g/1¹/₂ lb shoulder of veal, boned and cubed
300 ml/¹/₂ pt/1¹/₄ cups hot chicken stock
20 ml/4 tsp paprika
175 g/6 oz/3 cups button mushrooms
150 ml/¹/₂ pt/²/₃ cup soured (dairy sour) cream
30 ml/2 tbsp flaked almonds, lightly toasted

1 Place the bacon in a frying pan and fry in its own fat until crisp. Remove from the pan, add the butter and fry the onions until golden and soft – about 5 minutes.

2 Put the veal, bacon and onion in a 2 litre (3¹/₂ pt) casserole dish (Dutch oven). Pour over the stock, mixed with the paprika. Cover and cook for 45 minutes.

3 Add the mushrooms to the veal with the soured cream. Adjust the seasoning and stir gently.

4 Finish cooking. Sprinkle with the almonds and serve.

TEMP	TIME
150°C (no need to preheat) then: 150°C	45 minutes then: 30 minutes

LASAGNE

SERVES 4–6

✳

100 g/4 oz ready-to-use lasagne
10 g/¹/₂ oz/¹/₂ tbsp butter

For the meat sauce:
450 g/1 lb minced (ground) beef
1 garlic clove, crushed
3 streaky bacon rashers (slices)
1 large onion, chopped
Salt and freshly ground black pepper
2 carrots, grated
45 ml/3 tbsp tomato purée (paste)
300 ml/¹/₂ pt/1¹/₄ cups water
5 ml/ 1 tsp oregano
15 ml/1 tbsp Worcestershire sauce

For the cheese sauce:
50 g/2 oz/¹/₄ cup margarine
50 g/2 oz/¹/₂ cup plain (all-purpose) flour
600 ml/1 pt/2¹/₂ cups milk
175 g/6 oz/1¹/₂ cups strong Cheddar cheese, grated
Pinch of ground nutmeg
Freshly ground black pepper

1 Grease a 2.25 litre (4 pt) ovenproof dish with the butter.

2 Put all the ingredients for the meat sauce into a pan with a lid. Bring to the boil, stirring until thoroughly mixed. Reduce heat and simmer for 30 minutes.

3 Melt the margarine in a pan, stir in the flour then gradually blend in the milk off the heat. When the sauce is smooth return to the heat. Stir in two-thirds of the cheese and season with the nutmeg and black pepper.

4 Prepare the lasagne according to the instructions on the packet.

5 Spread a layer of meat sauce over the base of the dish. Place a layer of lasagne over the meat and another layer of meat sauce over the top. Cover with half the cheese sauce then another layer of lasagne.

6 Put the remaining meat sauce over this then a final layer of cheese sauce, trying to cover the meat completely.

7 Scatter the rest of the cheese on top. Bake.

TEMP	TIME
170°C (no need to preheat)	30–40 minutes or until brown on top

COOK'S NOTE
Once assembled the lasagne can be cooled then frozen. Defrost thoroughly before baking, then bake as follows: Temp: 160–170°C (not necessary to preheat) Time: 50–60 minutes.

Additional cooking functions if available (refer to your manufacturer's instructions for guidance:)

   OR

Suggested temp: 180–190°C or equivalent
Time: for the last 15–20 minutes of cooking to brown the topping

BŒUF EN CROUTE

SERVES 4–6

✳

900 g–1.5 kg/2–3 lb whole fillet of beef (preferably from the middle)
30 ml/2 tbsp olive oil
175 g/6 oz/3 cups button mushrooms, finely chopped
25–50 g/1–2 oz/2–4 tbsp butter
175 g/6 oz coarse liver pâté
15 ml/1 tbsp chopped fresh parsley
30–45 ml/2–3 tbsp brandy OR sherry
Salt and freshly ground black pepper
450 g/1 lb puff pastry (paste), ready-made, fresh or frozen
Beaten egg, for brushing

For the mushroom sauce:
40 g/1$^{1}/_{2}$ oz/3 tbsp butter
40 g/1$^{1}/_{2}$ oz/3 tbsp plain (all-purpose) flour
450 ml/$^{3}/_{4}$ pt/2 cups beef stock
A few drops of soy sauce
150 ml/$^{1}/_{4}$ pt/$^{2}/_{3}$ cup red wine
225 g/8 oz/4 cups mushrooms, wiped and sliced

➊ Trim the fillet and brush with oil. Place on a roasting grid above the drip tray and seal in the oven.

TEMP	TIME
200–220°C (preheat for 8 minutes)	15–20 minutes

➋ Remove from the oven, transfer to a cold dish and chill in the refrigerator loosely covered with foil, to cool as quickly as possible. Meanwhile, fry the mushrooms in the butter until soft, transfer to a bowl and allow to cool.

3. Mix together the pâté, herbs, mushrooms, brandy or sherry and salt and pepper.

4. Roll out the pastry to a rectangle long enough and wide enough to wrap the fillet completely (at least 3 times the width, twice the length).

5. Spread the pâté mixture down the centre and lay the chilled fillet on top.

6. Cut the corners off the pastry and reserve. Brush the exposed pastry with a little water. Fold in the ends, then fold in the sides and pinch the edges together to seal. Turn the parcel over and place on a baking sheet.

7. Brush all over with beaten egg. Roll out the remnants of the pastry thinly and cut leaf shapes, marking the veins with a knife. Stick on to the fillet parcel and brush with egg.

8. Snip 3 or 4 holes in the top of the pastry and bake. Leave to stand for 5 minutes before slicing.

TEMP	TIME
190–200°C (preheated for 5–8 minutes)	30–40 minutes (depending on the thickness of your fillet. Use your meat probe if you have one)

Additional cooking functions if available (refer to your manufacturer's instructions for guidance):

OR

Suggested temp: 190–200°C
Time: for the last 15–20 minutes
of cooking to dry and crisp
the base of the pastry

9 To make the mushroom sauce, melt the butter and stir in the flour. Gradually add the stock, stirring constantly, and bring to the boil.

10 Simmer gently, add the soy sauce, red wine and season to taste.

11 Add the mushrooms and cook until just tender.

12 Serve in a sauce boat along with the bœuf en croûte.

BEEF AND BEER CASSEROLE

COURTESY OF BOSCH (UK) LTD

SERVES 6

✳

1 kg/2¼ lb braising steak
25 g/1 oz/¼ cup plain (all-purpose) flour, seasoned
2 carrots
2 celery sticks
2 large onions
25 g/1 oz/2 tbsp butter OR dripping
5 ml/1 tsp chopped fresh parsley
Dash of Worcestershire sauce
Salt and freshly ground black pepper
225 g/8 oz/1 small can tomatoes
300 ml/ ½ pt/1¼ cups brown ale OR stout

1 Trim excess fat from the meat, cut into 2.5 cm (1 in) cubes and coat with flour.

2 Peel and slice the carrots, slice the celery and chop the onions.

3 Melt the fat and fry the meat and onions for about 5 minutes. Transfer the meat, vegetables, herbs, Worcestershire sauce and seasoning to a 1–1½ litre (2–3 pt) casserole dish (Dutch Oven).

4 Add the tomatoes and beer. Cover and bake.

TEMP	TIME
150°C (no need to preheat)	2–2½ hours, or until meat is tender

LIVER CASSEROLE

COURTESY OF ATAG (UK) LTD

SERVES 4

1 onion, sliced
25 g/1 oz/2 tbsp butter
450 g/1 lb lambs' liver, sliced
50 g/2 oz/1 cup fresh white breadcrumbs
15 ml/1 tbsp chopped fresh parsley
5 ml/1 tsp dried thyme
45 ml/3 tbsp shredded suet
Salt and freshly ground black pepper
Grated rind of $^{1}/_{2}$ lemon
Egg OR milk, to mix
4 streaky bacon rashers (slices)
300 ml/$^{1}/_{2}$ pt/1$^{1}/_{4}$ cups beef stock

1 Fry the onion in the butter until soft, transfer to a shallow casserole (Dutch Oven).

2 Slice the liver into 4 pieces and arrange on top of the onions.

3 Mix together the breadcrumbs, parsley, thyme, suet, seasoning and lemon rind and bind together with a little egg or milk.

4 Spread the stuffing on the liver and place a rasher of bacon on top of each slice. Pour in the stock and cover the casserole.

5 Cook, removing foil for the final 15 minutes to crisp the bacon.

TEMP	TIME
150°C	45–50 minutes (if preheated) OR 50–60 minutes (from cold)

CORNISH PASTIES

Being half Cornish I feel justified in including this recipe, which tastes better than any shop-bought pasty.

The pastry (paste) should be robust enough for the pasty to be eaten held in the hands with a serviette wrapped around the bottom. Please note, the genuine article does not include carrots, stock or flaky pastry.

This pastry uses less fat than standard shortcrust pastry (basic pie dough).

MAKES 4

✳

For the pastry:

100 g/4 oz/$^{1}/_{2}$ cup lard, well chilled

50 g/2 oz/$^{1}/_{4}$ cup margarine, well chilled

450 g/1 lb/4 cups plain (all-purpose) flour

Salt

Cold water, to bind

For the filling:

4 potatoes

2 small onions

450 g/1 lb lean beef

1 small turnip

25 g/2 oz/$^{1}/_{4}$ cup butter

Salt and white pepper to taste

Milk OR beaten egg, for brushing

1 To make the pastry, rub the fats into the flour until the mixture resembles fine breadcrumbs (this can be done in a food processor). Add the salt and enough water to form a soft dough.

2 Cover with clingfilm (plastic wrap) but DO NOT chill.

3 Peel the potatoes and peel and quarter the onions. Cover both with cold water in the same container until ready to use.

④ Trim any excess fat from the meat and dice into approximately 5 mm (¹/₄ in) pieces.

⑤ Divide the pastry into four equal pieces and roll out one piece into a circle 20–23 cm (8–9 in) in diameter. Hold an upturned dinner plate over the pastry to give a good circle.

⑥ Peel the turnip and cut into 4 pieces. Take one piece and slice into thin flakes on to the centre of the pastry circle, leaving a 5 cm (2 in) border all the way round.

⑦ Flake a potato on top of the turnip, keeping just a little back.

⑧ Thinly slice a quarter of the onion on top of the potato.

⑨ Put a quarter of the meat on top and cover with the remaining flaked potato.

⑩ Season well and put a small knob of butter on top.

⑪ Dampen the edges of the pastry with a little water, gently fold over one side, placing and pressing the edges together. (Don't worry if the filling moves as long as it's all tucked in when it comes to sealing the edges.)

⑫ Lift up the edges of the pastry and pinch together with the fingers and thumb of the left hand and fold over with the right hand to form a rope effect which, when released, will be on the curved edge of the pasty.

⑬ Make a small slit on top of the pasty to allow steam to escape.

⑭ Repeat steps 5 to 13 for the remaining three pasties.

⑮ Brush with the milk or beaten egg and put each pasty on a sheet of greaseproof (waxed) paper on a baking sheet.

⑯ Bake.

TEMP	TIME
190–200°C (preheat for 6–8 minutes) *then:* 180°C	20 minutes *then:* 40 minutes

COOK'S NOTE
Use two packets of bought shortcrust pastry to save time. The pasties can be frozen once cooked and cooled. Defrost thoroughly before eating cold or warmed for 20–30 minutes at 160–170°C.

Additional cooking function if available (refer to your manufacturer's instructions for guidance):

Suggested temp: 180–190°C
Time: for the first 20 minutes of cooking

MOUSSAKA

SERVES 6–8

✳

900 g/2 lb minced (ground) lamb
60 ml/4 tbsp tomato purée (paste)
300 ml/^{1}/$_2$ pt/1^1/$_4$ cups passata (sieved tomatoes)
5 ml/1 tsp chopped fresh parsley
2.5 ml/^{1}/$_2$ tsp dried thyme
2 garlic cloves, crushed
Dash of Worcestershire sauce
5 ml/1 tsp allspice
1 red onion, chopped
150 ml/^{1}/$_4$ pt/^{2}/$_3$ cup water
Salt and freshly ground black pepper
450 g/1 lb aubergines (eggplant), sliced
450 g/1 lb potatoes, sliced
Oil, for frying

For the sauce topping:
50 g/2 oz/^{1}/$_4$ cup butter
50 g/2 oz/^{1}/$_2$ cup plain (all-purpose) flour
600 ml/1 pt/2^1/$_2$ cups milk
175 g/6 oz/1^1/$_2$ cups Cheddar cheese, grated
2 eggs, separated
Freshly ground black pepper

1 Combine the lamb, tomato purée, passata, parsley, thyme, garlic, Worcestershire sauce, allspice, onion, water and seasoning in a saucepan and simmer steadily for 45 minutes, stirring occasionally. Allow to cool slightly and skim off any excess fat and surface deposits.

2 Sprinkle the aubergines with salt and leave for 30 minutes.

3 Meanwhile simmer or steam the sliced potatoes until slightly soft. Drain and transfer to a plate. Rinse and drain the aubergine slices and fry in the oil until golden.

4 Line a 2.25 litre (4 pt) casserole dish (Dutch Oven) with the aubergines. Pour over the meat mixture and arrange the potato slices over the meat.

5 Melt the butter and stir in the flour. Gradually add the milk and stir until thickened. Season with pepper and add the grated cheese. Cool slightly then stir in the egg yolks. Beat the egg whites, fold into the sauce and pour over the potatoes.

6 Bake.

TEMP	TIME
180°C	40–50 minutes

COOK'S NOTE
This dish can be prepared up to and including stage 5, chilled, then frozen. Defrost thoroughly before cooking and bake for 1½ hours.

SAUSAGE PLAIT

SERVES 4

✳

For the pastry (paste):
175 g/6 oz/³/₄ cup margarine
350 g/12 oz/3 cups plain (all-purpose) flour
Salt
Cold water, to bind

For the filling:
225 g/8 oz sausagemeat
110 g/4 oz/2 cups mushrooms, chopped
1 small onion, finely chopped
15 ml/1 tbsp chopped fresh parsley
Salt and freshly ground black pepper
Dash of Worcestershire sauce
Beaten egg, to glaze

1 Rub the fat into the flour and salt until the mixture resembles fine breadcrumbs. Add enough water to form a dough. Knead together gently. Roll out into a rectangle 30 × 38 cm (12 × 15 in).

2 Lightly mark three equal sections down the length of the pastry. Make diagonal cuts down each side section and dampen with a little water.

3 Mix all the filling ingredients together in a bowl and form into an oblong shape to fit into the centre section of the pastry, leaving 3.5 cm (1¹/₂ in) free at each end.

4 Starting from the top, bring the end of the pastry over the filling and fold alternate sides over the centre, forming a plait. Tuck the bottom end of the pastry over before overlapping the last two strips. (See diagram on page 135.)

5 Lift on to a lined baking sheet, brush with the beaten egg and bake.

6 Serve hot or cold.

TEMP	TIME
180°C	30–40 minutes (if preheated) OR 40–50 minutes (from cold)

COOK'S NOTE
350 g/12 oz ready-made pastry (paste) can be used to save time.

Additional cooking functions if available (refer to your manufacturer's instructions first):

 OR

Suggested temp: 190°C
Time: for the last 20 minutes of cooking to crisp the base

GARLIC BREAD

✳

1 large French stick OR baguette
100 g/4 oz/¹/₂ cup butter, softened
2 garlic cloves, crushed
5 ml/1 tsp dried mixed herbs
Salt and freshly ground black pepper

1 Slice the bread through in 5 cm (2 in) pieces.

2 Mix the garlic with the butter, herbs and seasoning.

3 Spread the mixture liberally on both sides of the chunks of bread. Put pieces back together to form two half baguettes.

4 Wrap each half well in foil and bake.

TEMP	TIME
170–190°C (the hotter the oven, the crisper the bread; choose the temperature which suits other food being cooked)	20–25 minutes (if preheated) OR 25–30 minutes (from cold)

Variations:

The garlic can be substituted with 15 ml/1 tbsp Dijon mustard or simply extra herbs and no garlic.

Cheesey Garlic Bread

Add 50 g/2 oz/¹/₂ cup grated Cheddar cheese and 50 g/2 oz/¹/₂ cup grated Gruyère cheese to the butter and garlic. Spread any leftover butter mixture on top of the bread and undo the foil for the last 10 minutes.

FARMHOUSE TERRINE

COURTESY OF ZANUSSI LTD

SERVES 8–10

✳

225 g/8 oz/1¹/₃ cups streaky bacon, rinded
2 bay leaves
225 g/8 oz/2 cups lambs' liver, minced
225 g/8 oz/2 cups lean pork, minced
1 small onion, finely chopped
50 g/2 oz/1 cup fresh breadcrumbs
Salt and freshly ground black pepper
Pinch of dried basil
1 garlic clove, crushed
1 egg, size 3, beaten
Dash of Worcestershire sauce

1 Stretch the bacon with the back of a knife.

2 Place the bay leaves in the botton of a 450 g (1 lb) loaf tin, then line the tin with the bacon. Trim off any overlapping bacon.

3 Finely chop any remaining bacon and add to the rest of the ingredients. Mix well.

4 Transfer the mixture to the lined loaf tin. Stand the tin in a roasting tin filled with water, lightly cover the top with foil and cook until the liquid runs clear when tested with a skewer.

6 When cool, tip out and leave in the refrigerator until cold.

TEMP	TIME
150°C (no need to preheat)	60–70 minutes

QUICHE LORRAINE

SERVES 6

✳

For the pastry (paste):

175 g/6 oz/1¹/₂ cups plain (all-purpose) flour

75 g/3 oz/¹/₃ cup block margarine

30 ml/2 tbsp approx. cold water

OR 225 g/8 oz ready-made shortcrust pastry (basic pie dough)

For the filling:

1 small onion, chopped

25 g/1 oz/2 tbsp margarine

100 g/4 oz streaky bacon

100 g/4 oz/1 cup strong Cheddar cheese, grated

3 eggs

300 ml/¹/₂ pt/1¹/₄ cups single (light) cream and milk, mixed

Pinch of cayenne pepper

Salt and freshly ground black pepper

Pinch of dried mixed herbs (optional)

Pinch of ground nutmeg

1 To make the pastry, rub the margarine into the flour with cool fingertips until it resembles fine breadcrumbs.

2 Add the cold water and gently bind together with a knife. Roll the pastry out to 3 mm (¹/₈ in) thickness and use to line a 20 cm (8 in) flan tin (pie shell).

3 Gently roll the rolling pin across the edge of the tin to neaten the pastry. Squeeze up the sides to allow for shrinkage during cooking.

4 Fry the onion in the margarine until soft, then spread on the pastry base.

5 Fry the bacon and cut into squares. Spread over the onion. Sprinkle three-quarters of the cheese over the bacon.

6 Beat the eggs in a basin, add the cream and milk and mix well. Add the cayenne pepper and seasoning. Pour over the bacon. Sprinkle the remaining cheese and the nutmeg on the top, place on a baking sheet and bake.

TEMP	TIME
190°C (preheat for 8 minutes) *then:* 160–170°C	20 minutes *then:* 20–25 minutes, until set and golden brown

COOK'S NOTE

A metal flan tin conducts the heat very quickly. If using a ceramic or earthenware dish bake the pastry blind first for 15–20 minutes.

Additional cooking functions if available (refer to your manufacturer's instructions for guidance):

          OR

Suggested temp: 170°C (not necessary to preheat)
Time: 35–40 minutes until set and golden brown

NB: There is no need to blind bake the pastry case first.

PIZZA

MAKES 1 VERY LARGE PIZZA

✳

For the base:
1 packet white bread mix

For the herby tomato filling:
400 g/14 oz/1 large can chopped tomatoes
45–60 ml/3–4 tbsp tomato purée (paste)
Good pinch of dried mixed herbs
Garlic salt (optional)
Salt and freshly ground black pepper

For the toppings:
100 g/4 oz salami
100 g/4 oz/1 cup Mozzarella cheese
$^1/_2$ green (bell) pepper, thinly sliced
100 g/4 oz/1 cup Cheddar cheese, grated
Mixed herbs, for sprinkling
Black olives, for decoration

1 Lightly grease a baking sheet then make up the bread mix according to the packet instructions.

2 Roll the dough out and place on the baking sheet. Spread more with your knuckles if necessary.

3 Drain the tomatoes of most of their juice and discard or store in the refrigerator for later use. Mix the tomatoes together with the other filling ingredients. Spread on the pizza base to within 1 cm ($^1/_2$ in) of the edge.

4 Slice the salami, Mozzarella and green pepper thinly and arrange attractively on the pizza. Sprinkle with the Cheddar cheese, mixed herbs and olives.

⑤ Leave for 30 minutes to rise again slightly.

⑥ Bake.

Alternative toppings:

50 g/2 oz/1 cup mushrooms, sliced
175 g/6 oz /1 small can tuna, drained and flaked
50 g/2 oz/$^1/_2$ cup sweetcorn (corn)
100 g/4 oz/1 cup ham, thinly sliced and cubed
100 g/4 oz/1 cup prawns (shrimp)

TEMP	TIME
190–200°C (preheat for 8 minutes)	25–30 minutes

Additional cooking functions if available:

Suggested temp: 190–200°C (preheated for 8 minutes)
Time: 25–30 minutes

     OR

Refer to your manufacturer's instructions for operating either of these functions.

DESSERTS

RHUBARB AND RASPBERRY CRUNCH LAYER

COURTESY OF BELLING APPLIANCES LTD

SERVES 6–8

✳

100 g/4 oz/$^1/_2$ cup butter, melted
100 g/4 oz/1 cup rolled oats
100 g/4 oz/1 cup digestive biscuits (Graham crackers) OR ginger biscuits, (cookies) coarsely crushed
50 g/2 oz/$^1/_2$ cup mixed chopped nuts
175 g/6 oz/$^3/_4$ cup demerara (light brown) sugar
Good pinch of ground cinnamon
450 g/1 lb rhubarb, cut into 2.5 cm (1 in) pieces
225 g/8 oz/1 cup frozen raspberries, defrosted

1 Mix the butter, oats, biscuits, nuts, half the sugar and cinnamon. In another bowl, mix the remaining sugar and fruits.

2 Place half the fruit in the bottom of a 1.2 litre (2 pt) casserole dish (Dutch oven). Sprinkle with half the biscuit mixture. Repeat with the remaining fruit followed by the biscuit mixture.

3 Bake.

TEMP	TIME
160–170°C	30–35 minutes (if preheated) OR 35–40 minutes (from cold)

BAKED APPLES

SERVES 4

※

4 firm eating (dessert) apples
15 ml/1 tbsp lemon juice
60 ml/4 tbsp mincemeat
1 egg white
50 g/2 oz/^{1}/$_4$ cup caster (superfine) sugar
2.5 ml/^{1}/$_2$ tsp ground cinnamon

1 Remove the apple cores with an apple corer, scraping out with a small sharp knife if necessary. Sprinkle a little lemon juice in each.

2 Make a slit around each apple. Use a teaspoon to put as much mincemeat as you can in the centre of each apple.

3 Place the apples in a shallow ovenproof dish, cover with foil and bake.

4 Meanwhile, whisk the egg white until stiff and gradually add the sugar until the meringue is thick and glossy. Spoon some over each apple, sprinkle with cinnamon and return to the oven.

TEMP	TIME
160°C (no need to preheat) *then:* 160°C (already hot)	1 hour *then:* 10 mins

FRUIT TART

COURTESY OF DIE DIETRICH

SERVES 6–8

For the pastry (paste):
100 g/4 oz/^{1}/$_2$ cup butter, softened

100 g/4 oz/^{1}/$_2$ cup caster (superfine) sugar

2 eggs

2.5 ml/^{1}/$_2$ tsp vanilla essence (extract)

225 g/8 oz/2 cups plain (all-purpose) flour

For the filling:
150 ml/^{1}/$_4$ pt/^{2}/$_3$ cup double (heavy) cream

2 eggs

25 g/1 oz/2 tbsp caster (superfine) sugar

2.5 ml/^{1}/$_2$ tsp vanilla essence (extract)

For the topping:
450 g/1 lb fresh apricots, stoned and quartered

OR 450 g/1 lb canned stoned cherries, drained

1 Make the pastry by beating together the butter, sugar, eggs and vanilla essence until smooth. Add the flour and knead lightly to a soft dough. Wrap and chill in the refrigerator for 1 hour.

2 Roll out the pastry and use to line a 23 cm (9 in) round or square flan tin (pie shell).

3 Whisk together all the filling ingredients.

4 Arrange the fruit in the pastry case, then pour the filling mixture over the top.

5 Stand the tin on a baking tray and bake.

TEMP	TIME
190°C (preheat for 5–8 minutes) *then:* 170°C	15 minutes *then:* 25–35 minutes, or until the custard is set and beginning to colour

COOK'S NOTES
Glaze the tart with a little apricot or cherry jam (conserve) when cool – if no one eats it first – it is delicious warm! To save time you could use a packet of fresh or frozen pastry for the base.

Alternative cooking functions if available (refer to your manufacturer's instructions for guidance):

 OR

Suggested temp: 170–180°C
Time: 35–40 minutes

May also be used if available for last 20 minutes only.

FRENCH APPLE OR PEAR FLAN

SERVES 8

✳

For the pastry (paste):

225 g/8 oz/2 cups plain (all-purpose) flour, sifted

100 g/4 oz/^{1}/$_2$ cup butter

15 ml/1 tbsp icing (confectioners') sugar

1 egg yolk

30 ml/2 tbsp cold water

For the filling:

100 g/4 oz/^{1}/$_2$ cup butter

100 g/4 oz/^{1}/$_2$ cup caster (superfine) sugar

1 egg, beaten

1 egg yolk

15 ml/1 tbsp Calvados OR brandy

100 g/4 oz/^{1}/$_2$ cup ground almonds

30 ml/2 tbsp plain (all-purpose) flour

2–3 drops almond essence (extract)

3–4 dessert (eating) apples OR pears

30–45 ml/2–3 tbsp apricot jam (conserve), to glaze

① Rub the butter into the flour until the mixture resembles fine breadcrumbs.

② Stir in the icing sugar and bind together with the egg yolk and water. Knead lightly into a ball and allow to rest in a refrigerator for 30 minutes.

③ Meanwhile cream the butter and sugar together until light and fluffy.

④ Add the egg and yolk a little at a time, beating well between each addition.

5 Stir in the Calvados, ground almonds, flour and almond essence.

6 Roll out the pastry to line a 25 cm (10 in) flan tin (pie shell). Prick the base lightly and spread the almond mixture evenly over the base.

7 Halve and peel the apples. Remove the core carefully. Place each apple half face down on a board and slice through thinly, holding the slices together. Fan out so that the slices are overlapping and place on to the almond mixture in a line from the centre of the flan. Press down firmly but gently into the mixture. Repeat for the remaining apples arranging the lines of slices like the spokes of a wheel (see page 10 for picture).

8 Bake.

9 Brush with apricot glaze (see page 177) before serving.

TEMP	TIME
180–190°C (preheat for 5–8 minutes) *then:* 160-170°C	15 minutes *then:* 20–30 minutes, until the apples are soft and the filling set

Alternative cooking functions if available (refer to your manufacturer's instructions):

 Temperature and time as given in recipe

OR

Suggested temp: 190–200°C or equivalent as given in your manufacturer's instructions
Time: for the last 20 minutes of cooking

CHEESECAKE

SERVES 10

✳

100 g/4 oz/¹/₂ cup butter
225 g/8 oz/2 cups digestive biscuits (Graham crackers), crushed
700 g/1¹/₂ lb/3 cups curd (smooth cottage) cheese
3 eggs
15 ml/1 tsp vanilla essence (extract)
Lemon juice to taste
225 g/8 oz/1 cup caster (superfine) sugar
1 × 450 g/1 lb can cherry pie filling
150 ml/¹/₄ pt/²/₃ cup double (heavy) cream, whipped

1 Melt the butter and stir in the crushed digestive biscuits. Press into the base of a 20 cm (8 in) loose-bottom tin.

2 Beat the cheese, eggs, vanilla essence, lemon juice and sugar together until smooth and creamy.

3 Pour the mixture into the biscuit base. Sit the tin on a sheet of foil and then on a baking tray. Press the foil up around the side of the tin to prevent too much butter seeping on to the tray.

4 Bake. At the end of the cooking time turn the oven off and allow the cheesecake to cool in the oven.

5 Chill. Top with the cherries to within 2.5 cm (1 in) of the edge. Pipe rosettes of whipped cream around this edge to prevent the filling running over. Decorate the top with any remaining cream.

TEMP	TIME
130°C (from cold or preheated)	40 minutes approximately

FRUIT CRUMBLE

COURTESY OF TRICITY BENDIX

SERVES 6

✳

For the topping:
75 g/3 oz/¹/₃ cup butter
175 g/6 oz/1¹/₂ cups plain (all-purpose) flour
50 g/2 oz/¹/₄ cup demerara (light brown) sugar
50 g/2 oz/¹/₂ cup nuts, chopped
Grated rind of 1 lemon

For the filling:
450 g/1 lb fruit (rhubarb, apples, pears etc.)
75 g/3 oz/¹/₃ cup sugar

1 Grease a 1 litre (2 pt) dish, chop the fruit, place in the dish and add the sugar.

2 Rub the fat into the flour until the mixture resembles fine breadcrumbs. Add the sugar, nuts and lemon rind.

3 Sprinkle over the fruit. Bake.

TEMP	TIME
190°C	35–40 minutes (if preheated) OR 40–45 minutes (from cold)

MINCEMEAT AND MARZIPAN JALOUSIE

SERVES 6–8

❊

450 g/1 lb frozen or fresh puff pastry (paste)
1 packet bought marzipan (almond paste)
450 g/1 lb/1¹/₃ cups mincemeat
2 tbsp brandy
1 egg, beaten
Icing (confectioners') sugar, for dredging

1 Cut the pastry in half and roll one piece to a rectangle approximately 15 × 30 cm (6 × 12 in). Place on a baking sheet.

2 Roll out the marzipan 2.5 cm (1 in) smaller all round than the pastry and lay on the pastry. (Don't worry if it breaks, just cover the pastry as best you can, it will not be seen).

3 Mix the brandy with the mincemeat and spread over the marzipan, leaving the pastry edge uncovered.

4 Roll out the second piece of pastry to the same size as the first. Fold in half lengthways and cut slits into the fold 1 cm (¹/₂ in) apart down the centre, leaving 5 cm (2 in) round the unfolded edge. Open out and place on top of the mincemeat.

5 Press the edges of the two pieces of pastry together firmly, then flake with the back of a knife to seal. Scallop the rim with your forefinger and the sharp edge of a knife.

6 Brush the top with beaten egg. Bake. Dredge with icing sugar and serve hot with whipped cream or ice cream.

TEMP	TIME
190–200°C (preheat for 5–8 minutes)	25 minutes, or until risen and golden brown

Alternative cooking functions if available (refer to your manufacturer's instructions):

Suggested temp: 190–200°C (not necessary to preheat)
Time: 25 minutes

OR

Suggested temp: 200–220°C (preheated for 10–15 minutes)
Time: 25 minutes

CHOCOLATE ROULADE

SERVES 6–8

✳

225 g/8 oz/1 cup caster (superfine) sugar
5 eggs, separated
40 g/1½ oz/3 tbsp cocoa (unsweetened chocolate powder), sifted

For the filling:
175 g/6 oz dark (semi-sweet) dessert chocolate
300 ml/½ pt/⅔ cup double (heavy) cream
Drops of brandy OR other liqueur
Icing (confectioners') sugar, for dusting

1 Grease and line a Swiss (jelly) roll tin with non-stick baking parchment. Lightly grease the paper all over as well.

2 Mix the sugar, egg yolks and cocoa together thoroughly.

3 Whisk the egg whites in a separate bowl until very stiff.

4 Stir approximately one third of the egg white into the cocoa mixture, then fold this gently into the bowl of egg white using a metal spoon.

5 Pour the mixture into the tin, gently tipping the mixture into the corners.

6 Bake. Remove from the oven and allow to cool in the tin for 2–3 minutes (no longer).

7 Break up the chocolate and melt either in a bowl over a saucepan of hot, but not boiling, water or on the low setting of a microwave.

⑧ Tip the roulade out gently on to a sheet of greaseproof (waxed) paper. Peel off the lining paper.

⑨ Spread the melted chocolate very gently over the warm roulade with a palette knife. Allow to cool and the chocolate to set slightly.

⑩ Whip the cream until peaking, stir in the brandy. Spread the cream over the roulade.

⑪ Roll up the roulade from the short end, using the paper to help the rolling. Place straight on to a serving dish. (Don't worry if the roulade cracks and sticks a little to the paper).

⑫ Chill. Dust with icing sugar just before serving. Decorate with whipped cream if wished.

TEMP	TIME
160–170°C (preheat for 5–8 minutes)	20–25 minutes

COOK'S NOTE
This freezes well. Roll straight on to a clean sheet of waxed paper, roll up in this and fold over the ends. Cover with freezer film and freeze.

BAKED ALASKA

COURTESY OF MIELE LTD

SERVES 6–8

225 g/8 oz/1 cup fresh or frozen raspberries
OR 225 g/7 oz/1 small can favourite fruit, drained
30 ml/2 tbsp orange-flavoured liqueur
1 × 20 cm (8 in) baked sponge flan
4 egg whites
175 g/6 oz/³/₄ cup caster (superfine) sugar
450 ml/³/₄ pt block vanilla ice cream

1 Place the raspberries on a shallow dish and sprinkle the liqueur over. Cover and leave for 2 hours, turning occasionally.

2 Place the sponge on a large ovenproof dish and spoon over the raspberries and juice.

3 Whisk the egg whites until stiff. Add 60 ml/4 tbsp of the sugar and whisk. Then fold in the remaining sugar gently until no traces remain.

4 Place the ice cream on the sponge and spoon (or pipe through a large nozzle) the meringue on top. Make sure the sponge and the ice cream are completely covered.

5 Bake until the meringue is tinged with brown and serve immediately.

TEMP	TIME
200–210°C (preheat for 8 minutes)	3–5 minutes

Alternative cooking function if available (refer to your manufacturer's instructions):

Suggested temp: 220°C if variable (preheated for 10–15 minutes)
Time: 3–5 minutes

PEACHES IN PUFF PASTRY

SERVES 8–12

❋

1 packet puff pastry (paste)
225 g/7 oz/1 small can peach halves in fruit juice
30 ml/2 tbsp apricot jam (conserve), for glazing

1 Cut the pastry in half and roll each piece into a rectangle 3 mm ($^1/_8$ in) thick and approximately 10 cm (4 in) wide. Lay next to each other on a baking sheet.

2 Drain the peaches and arrange down the length of the pastry, leaving a space of 2.5 cm (1 in) between each peach half.

3 Scallop the edge of the pastry all round with the fingers and the back of a knife.

4 Brush the exposed pastry with beaten egg. Bake.

5 Remove and brush with warm apricot glaze. Serve with whipped cream.

TEMP	TIME
190–200°C (preheat for 5–8 minutes)	20 minutes

COOK'S NOTE
To make the glaze, put 2 parts water to 1 part jam, warm gently, then sieve the mixture.

Alternative cooking function if available (refer to your manufacturer's instructions):

Suggested temp: 190–200°C (not necessary to preheat)
Time: 20–25 minutes

ALMOND TART

SERVES 6–8

✳

225 g/8 oz ready-made shortcrust pastry (basic pie dough)

For the filling:

1 tbsp raspberry jam (conserve)

100 g/4 oz/^{1}/$_2$ cup butter, softened

100 g/4 oz/^{1}/$_2$ cup caster (superfine) sugar

2 eggs, beaten

25 g/1 oz/2 tbsp self-raising (self-rising) flour

100 g/4 oz/1 cup ground almonds

Few drops of almond essence (extract)

50 g/2 oz/^{1}/$_3$ cup icing (confectioners') sugar

50 g/2 oz/^{1}/$_2$ cup flaked almonds

1 Roll out the pastry and use to line a 25 cm (10 in) flan tin (pie shell) or a Swiss (jelly) roll tin. Bake blind.

TEMP	TIME
190–200°C (preheated for 5–8 minutes)	15–20 minutes (remove baking beans for the last 5 minutes to allow the pastry to dry out)

2 Spread a little jam over the base of the pastry.

3 Cream the butter and sugar together until light and fluffy.

4 Add the eggs a little at a time.

5 Stir in the flour, almonds and almond essence.

6 Pour into the pastry case and bake.

7 Remove from the oven. Mix the icing sugar with enough water to make thin icing and pour and over the top. Sprinkle with the flaked almonds. Return to the oven.

TEMP	TIME
160–170°C (preheat for 8 minutes) *then:* 190–200°C (already hot)	35 minutes or until brown and firm to the touch. *then:* 5 minutes

Alternative cooking functions if available (refer to your manufacturer's instructions):

Suggested temp: 190°C (not necessary to preheat)
Time: 15 minutes

THEN

Suggested temp: 160–170°C
Time: 25–30 minutes

There is no need to blind bake pastry case if using either of these functions.

BREAD AND BUTTER PUDDING

SERVES 4–6

50 g/2 oz/2 tbsp butter
4 large slices bread and butter
50 g/2 oz/^{1}/$_3$ cup sultanas (golden raisins) OR raisins
3 eggs
40 g/1^1/$_2$ oz/3 tbsp caster (superfine) sugar
150 ml/^{1}/$_4$ pt/^{2}/$_3$ cup single (light) cream
450 ml/^{3}/$_4$ pt/2 cups milk
5 ml/1 tsp sugar
1.5 ml/^{1}/$_4$ tsp ground nutmeg
1.5 ml/^{1}/$_4$ tsp ground cinnamon

1 Butter a deep ovenproof dish.

2 Cut the crusts from the bread and butter and cut the slices into triangles.

3 Place alternate layers of bread and sultanas or raisins in the dish.

4 Beat together the eggs, caster sugar and cream.

5 Heat the milk to just under boiling point. Pour into the egg mixture, beating well.

6 Pour the milk mixture over the bread and dried fruit and allow to stand for 30 minutes. Sprinkle the sugar, nutmeg and cinnamon over the top.

TEMP	TIME
170°C (preheat for 8 minutes)	40 minutes approx.

COOK'S NOTE
Vary this by using brown bread and brown caster sugar.

PLATE APPLE PIE

SERVES 6–8

✳

900 g/2 lb Bramley (tart) apples
Squeeze of lemon juice
450 g/1 lb shortcrust pastry (basic pie dough)
Juice of $^1/_2$ orange
100 g/4 oz/$^1/_2$ cup sugar
2.5 ml/$^1/_2$ tsp ground cinnamon
Milk, for brushing
Sugar, for sprinkling

1 Peel, core and quarter the apples and cover with water to which a dash of lemon juice has been added.

2 Line a pie plate or shallow heatproof dish with one third of the pastry.

3 Slice the apples on to the pastry and sprinkle with orange juice, sugar and cinnamon. Dampen the edges of the pastry with water.

4 Roll out the remaining pastry large enough to overlap the top of the pie by 1 cm ($^1/_2$ in). Fold in half and make 3 diagonal slits on the fold. Open out and place on top of the apples.

5 Seal the edges, trim off the surplus pastry and pinch the edges together to form a decorative pattern.

6 Brush lightly with milk, sprinkle with a little sugar and bake.

TEMP	TIME
190°C (preheat for 5–8 minutes) *then:* 175°C	15 minutes *then:* 35 minutes

Alternative cooking functions if available (refer to your manufacturer's instructions):

  OR

Temperature and time as in recipe

THEN

Suggested temp: 200°C (if variable)
Time: for the last 20 minutes of cooking to crisp the base

PAVLOVA

SERVES 6–8

❋

4 egg whites
225 g/8 oz/1 cup caster (superfine) sugar
5 ml/1 tsp vanilla essence (extract)
5 ml/1 tsp cornflour (cornstarch)
5 ml/1 tsp vinegar
300 ml/¹/₂ pt/1¹/₄ cups double (heavy) cream
450 g/1 lb seasonal fresh soft fruit

1 Spread two sheets of non-stick parchment paper on two baking sheets. Draw one circle approximately 25 cm (10 in) in diameter and one circle approximately 18 cm (7 in) in diameter on the paper.

2 Whisk the egg whites in a large clean bowl until stiff (a palette knife sliced through should show a firm close texture and come out clean).

3 Add the sugar 1 teaspoonful at a time, whisking between each addition. If the sugar is added too quickly it will not be dissolved and will seep out during cooking.

4 Stir in the vanilla essence, cornflour and vinegar.

5 Spoon the mixture inside the circles on the baking parchment to form the base and 'lid' of the pavlova. Use the back of the spoon to shape into attractive swirls. The smaller circle can be left in soft peaks as this will be the 'lid'.

6 Bake. At the end of the cooking time turn off and allow to cool in the oven.

6 Place the base of the pavlova on a suitable serving plate.

7 Whip the cream and carefully spread half of this over the base. Arrange some fruit on top. Place the lid on and spoon the rest of the cream on the top and arrange the remaining fruit attractively on top of the cream.

TEMP	TIME
130–140°C (preheat for 8 minutes) *then:* 110–120°C	15 minutes *then:* 45 minutes

LEMON MERINGUE PIE

SERVES 6–8

❋

175 g/6 oz ready-made shortcrust pastry (basic pie dough)
60 ml/4 level tbsp cornflour (corn starch)
300 ml/^{1}/$_2$ pt/1^1/$_4$ cups water
25 g/1 oz/2 tbsp butter
Grated rind and juice of 2 lemons
225 g/8 oz/1 cup caster (superfine) sugar
2 eggs, separated

1 Roll out the pastry and use to line a deep 18–20 cm (7–8 in) flan case (pie shell). Prick the base, line with greaseproof (waxed) paper and put in rice or baking beans. Blind bake, removing the beans and greaseproof paper for the last 5 minutes. Leave to cool.

2 Blend the cornflour to a paste with a little of the cold water. Bring the butter and the rest of the water to the boil and pour over the blended cornflour, stirring well. Pour back into the pan and cook for 3 minutes, stirring all the time.

3 Remove from the heat and stir in the lemon rind and juice and half the sugar. Allow to cool a little.

4 Stir in the egg yolks and pour the mixture into the flan case.

5 Whisk the egg whites until stiff, add half the remaining sugar and whisk again until stiff. Fold in the remaining sugar and pile on top of the lemon mixture, gently spreading it right to the edge of the pastry.

6 Bake until the meringue is firm and lightly browned.

TEMP	TIME
190–200°C (preheat for 5–8 minutes) *then:* 140°C (already hot)	15–20 minutes *then:* 20–30 minutes (if serving warm) OR 40 minutes (if serving cold)

Alternative cooking function if available (refer to your manufacturer's instructions for guidance):

Suggested temp: 190–200°C (not necessary to preheat)
Time: 15–20 minutes

May be used for blind baking of the pastry case

INDEX